Phrases 2 Amaze 1's Curiosity

Thomas Bryan, JR

Kingdom Builders Publications LLC

Phrases 2 Amaze 1's Curiosity

Kingdom Builders Publications

Paperback ISBN –978-0-692-12940-1
Library of Congress Control Number – 2018950358

Cover Designer
Thomas Bryan, JR

Editor
Kingdom Builders Publications
Louise Smith

Photographer
Selah Bryan

Printed in USA

Send correspondences to:
Spagnitive1892@gmail.com or kbpublications@sc.rr.com

INTRODUCTION

I started writing this poetry book from a remark I made. I thought I could write

rhymes as good as some of the rappers known today, and could top the charts with my lyrics. While making that point, I figured out another point.

Growing up in the low country, I was always fascinated by tall tales and stories, history, Biblical stories, fairytale, folklore, fantasy, and fiction. I love listening to stories and could listen to them all day. They seem to have hidden messages and key mysteries in them; particularly in prose and poetry.

It is my belief that certain people I know living on Hilton Head Island have mysteries. Usually, when they would share their stories and knowledge, they would leave something out for me to wonder about and no story was ever told the same way twice, though the same story would change with each teller.

When I would retell a story, I find myself doing the same thing; changing the scene and words to my level of thinking. I discovered this about myself; telling any stories or tales would mean changing my level of thinking. This put me on a mission of reading about everything...social, political, science, health, religion, history of the living and the strolls of the dead, art, nature, hieroglyphics, signs, and stars. I became increasingly hungry to find the facts of my life.

Based on my journey, I know why I write poems and short stories. The journey of a low country man, who has observed the whole of life through reading, caring, and over-standing my meaning to live, helping another human being see a little more light.

My vision is to share some things I've learned from life's experiences, as an Black American man, who firmly believes in the "clean hands" man! My writing aims toward circumstances of the adult and young adult, Black men and women in the US. My goal is to bring forth more understanding to our situation. Home in America... and my identification to the Fatherland Africa.

All thanks to our Father, FATHER OF ALL I WRITE.

CHARM AND BLISS

I found a shell
While riding a boat
How lucky
Was I and I
To have found this shell
I put this shell
Up to my ear
And oh what wonderful words
How dear
Could this not be luck
But maybe a blessing
Or maybe
You are my life time lesson
I put this shell
Up to my chest
And it tells my heart
Be peaceful
Be careful
You are the best
I will always keep
My shell
Close to my faith
Close as my charm
And forever in my rest
Because my shell
You are the best

SUNKEN POSSIBILITY

It's October the 31st
Halloween
Creepy is the scene
Blood seekers
Lurks the lanes
Crawling through the room
Hear the witches scream
The sound
Of fear and doom
Of torture, hurt and pain
Where the wicked
Air looms
In the dark
Eyes creep
Creatures roam
Releases their horrible schemes
Howling at the moon
Zombies and blood thirsty fiends
Leaping from their tomb
Pumpkin-heads looking;
Looking mighty mean
So scary
Beware of the goons
Little children
On Halloween
Be careful
What you're letting
In your home
ooooooooooooh

PLAY BALL

It is October
And the season
Is over
For all the summer ballers
that couldn't
Get over
Playoff time
The time to grind
Diamonds
In the chalk lines
Second string
On the pine
The batter up
Gets the sign
Home run fence
Is 499
Pitch your arms doing fine
Make that curve
Swing from behind
Center fielders
Out there dying
Hit one there
And he'll go flying
The bat catchers
Behind it all
Catch the third one
Batters fall
Miss the target and
Across the walls
Third baseman gets the call
First baseman

Scoops it all
Short stop
Get the hop
Throw it to home
Make the stop
Second then third
Make that pop
Clean up hitter
Go for it all
Right field sprinter
Walks the wall
Left field cut off
Center relay the ball
Runners going home
It's going to be
A close call
When the pitcher gets pitching
The high speed ball
From the mound
To the mitten
October in the fall
It is playoff time
Let's play ball

FROM WHENCE I CAME

Where do I
Go from here
The tallest car
The biggest chair

Where do I
Go from here
The brightest star
A shining career
Where I'm going far
Hits prepared

Where do I
Go from here
Green stuffed cigar
And the carpets red
Where I'm
Black as tar
With gold coated
Pencil led

Where do I
Go from here
Back to Jah
Because fame
Will kill me dead
Where?

CHECK

In the poetry contest in the world
Who's the best?
Let us just roll out the chess
Now, what is your request?
To put me through the test?
If I'm better than the rest
Can I reach up
Under the dress?
Can I reach down
The one the less?
Can I make someone confess?
A poetry contest
Judge
What is your request
Can I capture
The scenes of the west?
Will it be
Hard on the chest
Or will I just
Be called a pest
Write about all dem mess
The stuff hidden up
Under the desk
All about
The people's stress
In the poetry contest
In the world
Who is the best
Let us just
Roll out the chess

FLAG

I wish
I were a butterfly
With wings
As wide as me
I'll float around
From tree to tree
and tell the world
All I see
Red gold and green
My colors will be
I'll glide
Upon the winds
Patiently
Across the open sea
I'll spread my colors
All over this earth
I'll bring back liberty

EARTH LINES

Are we
Living in borrowed time?
Have we
Crossed all of nature's lines?
ignored all
Instructional signs
Are we able to see?
But still yet still blind
Why can't we hear the plea?
Of the earth
The earthlings are crying
Like babies are giving birth
The gardens are dying
Could it be our worth?
Are we causing
Our world to decline
While we still multiply
Like wild southern pine?
Not identifying
With disasters left behind
Crossing all of
Jah
Border lines
We must seek together
In order to find
A cure for what
Is ours together
A common sense of mind
To save mankind
We are living on borrowed time!

JABS COMING IN

I'm coming in this ring
With a hook and a jab
Hitting everything
Coming in; you better grab
Right left sting send you to the lab
All you can bring, I'll put it on your tab
When you sing, gonna get you with the jab
When you swing
Duck uppercut
Dab
When the bell rings
Sock you with the jab
Ring
I am the king
Call me K.O. fab
Arrange everything
Put you in rehab
Coming in the ring
Straight out city cab
Wearing my bling
I earned it
With the jab
I'm coming in
You better duck
Dip or dab
You're falling
Player you better grab
Coming in
Rehab

BARS/ GATES/ FENCES

Not about vanity
All about humanity
Is togetherness insanity?
Would not unity take away the worry?
Humanity is a word that expresses us
Oneness!
How did it become two, three, or four
The less?
Five all in stress divided,
And the gate keepers never rest.
Together we quest
Together all confess
Don't let vanity bring apart humanity
We have failed the stress test
We are all locked up
Jailed
Under arrest
Bars gates fences
East/slash/west

PEACE

I share my love
With you
my wishes are
for no harm to come to you
All of your days
And for you to be
My friend
Each and every day
Always free
Be your way
All you meet
Be friendly to you
Prosperity and good health
Family love
And lots of wealth
Be in your days
Each and everyone
I share my love with you
Peace be unto you

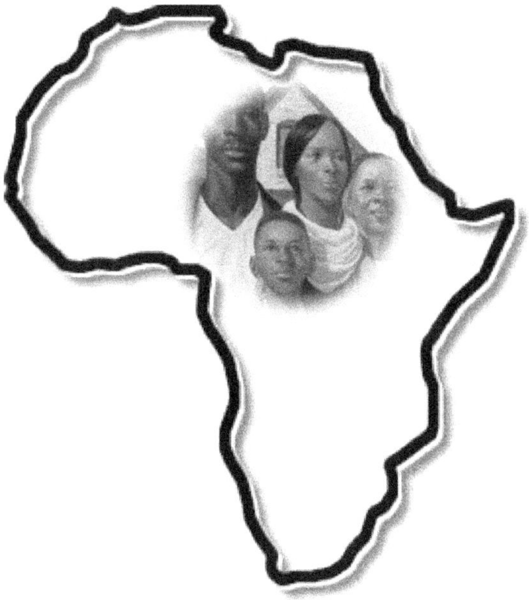

WHO'S BACK

Under attack
From the back
Somebody's selling crack
Somebody's holding back
Everybody
Is not slack
Somebody is on smack
Any body
Knows about that
Somebody talking whack
Everybody
We are black
Time somebody
Say the fact
Somebody's holding us back
Nobody knows the
Mack
But somebody's
Selling us crack
Somebody's bringing
The stacks
Everybody's under
Attack
The ships that sail
The hood men lack
Its planes
You can see
Warehouse packed
Somebody's selling us
Smack
Nobody knows
Who is in the back

Every body's got
A sack
Anybody knows
The fact
Who's been selling
The poor man crack
Now everybody's
Under attack
From the back

UP OR DOWN

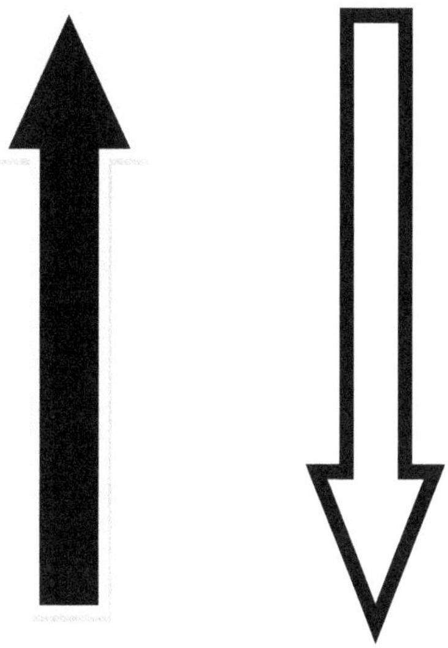

Are you up
With this world?
What is happening
To it today?
Are you up
With this world?
The games you lose
Dem play
Are you up
With this world?
Hear what
Leaders do not say
Are you up
With this world?
Disappointed alright or gay
Are you up
With this world?
Know this
The head leads
Tails obey
You up with this

Turning right
Or left way
You up with this
Are the children happy
Dear
O.k.
Are you up
With this world?
Are we here to blow
Or to stay?
Up with this world?
Because
If you are down with it
Just yield,
Kneel
Back up and pray!

JAH CURE

When the time comes
For the young lion
Who roars
Hatred and fear
Shall be no more!
Drugs and warfare
Would have to go
Disease and nuclear
The beast
Will cease to grow
The unholy
And despair
The truth?
Will truly show
In the pollution filled
Atmosphere
Remembering
The ark and the rainbow?
Their sickness
Is spreading everywhere
The heed is now
For the cure.
Young lions roar
Babylon release the cure.

STREET HEATER

The city streets
Are so damn cold
Hate getting
Out of control
Food is being taken
From the children's bowl
Nothing comes
Or goes for free
Everything stolen
Credit or sold
Here the bluff
There's always fear
The good man always fold
The streets are over run by the young
Their biggest fight are the old
Where the most important code is
To wear more than you're worth
In shoes and in gold
Every player reaches the key
Thinks he is the one that breaks the mold
Starts to kill
Out of control
Makes them hate him
Wants to see him
In a hole
Fathers not taking
Care of their own
But always down
With the street's own
When it's time
To roll

Living in the city
Their life is freeze cold
The only thing you've got
Is your self-control
Gotta watch your back
Just taking a stroll
All hate no love
Like the 1949
Rush for gold
You cannot trust
A living soul
Every person out for self
Doing for self only
And never as a whole
When selfish goes down
No help
That is out of the hole
Police treat everyone
Like dealers and hoes
Claiming they are only
Keeping control
What they're saying
We're guilty
Their files are closed
Fold
There's no good way out
Of this cold, cold, hole;
Our respected holy men
Have fallen
To self-temptation
And the love of gold
Our virtuous women
Are getting tired and old
The educated children

Are not looking back
Too much for them
To behold
No one helping him out
Out of the ghetto
The stories of solution
Remain untold
Hate rules the day
All whom have something
Have not a soul
Treating the poor poorly
Not equally
Until their votes are needed
At the poles
Like I said
From the bottom to the top
The whole damn world
Is so damn cold
Love is on the drop
And the rising of peace
Has stopped
The good are getting old
People worshiping
Themselves these days
And what's left
They give to gold
The place is very cold
Street heater

ROOTS

My roots go deep within the earth
It lies through history
It crawls and creeps in stores
My family ties
My grands
It holds and keep for the future
Won't be denied
When curiosity begins to peep
On a branch of the tree from up high
Its fruit begin to leap into the harvest
As the future goes by
It's your roots
Our heritage you seek
So that you can reach the peak
A family tie
Grows deep mama
Grows high papa
Roots
Creeps
Deep

WORD UP

Action speaks louder than words
A-c-t-i-o-n
Every damn syllable heard
Put it in motion
Make it a fortune
Fly just like a bird
Patient and devotion
At the table of life
Get a healthy portion
When action speaks loudly,
Clear is the word
Seven days a week
The songs of action is heard
When the talker finishes the talk
The walker finishes the walk
Action!
Always in front of the herd
And when the flocker starts to flock
Flock on a clock
Steady is the action bird
I want to buy it
Until you fly it
Action speaks louder than words

A ambitious able
C courageously cooperative
T timing timely
I intelligence independent
O obedience obeisance
N nice nature

…Speaks louder than words

U.S.

The great man dreamed
about us
He dreamed
The American dream
Would mean us
He dreamed
Holding hands
Would be us
He dreamed
Positive characters
Will be us
He dreamed
Struggling together
Would be us
He dreamed
Stones of hopes
To be us
He dreamed
Sweet land of liberty
Would embrace us
He dreamed
Symphony of brotherhood
Means us
Working and playing together
For us
He dreamed
Let freedom ring
He dream us
He was a king
He dreamed
United states
He meant us

TASTE DA FAITH

A whiskey on Sunday morning
Getting ready to hear the warning
In the church
Faith is dawning
Every one's in there phoning
Everything except the warning
Preacher singing
Pastors yarning
Deacons hanging around the skirting
Sisters got a thing
Brothers hurting
A whiskey on Sunday morning
Getting ready to hear the warning

SPACE RACE

Oh yes they came from out of space
They were all heartless and broke
So their ship was parked
At the free base
Their whole planet was a total waste
From the free base
They started a new race with a glass horn
Orbiting minds up
Lost in space
Leaving a dreadful sink in their face
Lawyers on their case
Blow guns packed with poisonous lace
When hit you move
In a blurry eye haste
Enter the rat chase
Mincing away your grace
Taking up just space from the free base
Cracked open the rock case
Out came a new race
Cold blooded and sunken face
They landed on the free base
They planned it for a total waste
It is an unidentified flying object
Dem master case

REST IN PEACE

The forbidden word
Trigger
With the hidden verb
That triggers
Pinches nerves
You're bigger
how does the server
Figures
When dem up
And call you
Trigger
Will it be deserved
If said by white
Figure
You jump like
Tigger
If said by black
Figure
Oh that's kool
Jigger
Let us kill
And bury
The mixed-up word
Trigger
And leave it
To the dead
And the zombie
Hate digger

POPPY EYES

Mrs. Meth
Crystal, crystal
You're so fine
Liquid pistol
Held to the mind
Blowing your whistle
robbing blind
When she hits you
Stop
You in time
Leaving a meth
On your mind
Sends your body
Into time
Far behind
Beyond mankind
Have you thinking
Crystal shine
Liquid pistol
Held to the mind
You pull the trigger
Every time
Blowing out
Your conscious mind
Leaving just
A body behind
Mrs. Meth heroin

PAIN KILLER

Reach for my Hennessey
Thinking about my enemy
War
Hate
Jealousy
Instigate
False policy
Exaggerate
Documentary of
Bias debate
The poor misery
Reaching for my Hennessy
Two
Thinking about my poverty
Thinking about
The effects on me
Seeing the child
Of a poor family
Sensing the wild
Becoming history
Reaching for my Hennessy
Three
Thinking about
How it used to be
Stepping
Straight out of chain
Slavery
Walking
Straight into
White society
Following a star

Into the inner city
Scattered about
Looking for the free
Without a doubt
Reaching for my Hennessy
Four
Trying to break the drought
Of the pain
Inside of me
While thinking about
My entire hated enemy
Envy
Jealousy
Misery
Slavery
Poverty
And the false prophecy
In humanity
My Hennessy

ONE EQUALS ONE

I'm just a man
You can see
I've got human being
Written all over me
I over stand humanity
But don't understand
Superiority
More than a man
Can eye see
Is more than a man
Luxury
Is more than a man
The most holy
Is more than a man
Just happy
Is more than a man
Misery
Is more than a man
Murderously
Is there a man here
Jah loves
Better than me
Humanly?

NO PROBLEM

I write of that problem
That is every one's problem
Relationship problem
Money problem
Work problem
Family problem
Friendship problem
Country problem
Neighborhood problem
Man problem
Women problem
Love problem
Hate problem
Rate problem
Gun problem
Drug problem
Hunger problem
Decease problem
Justice problem
School problem
Crime problem
Rule problem
Time problem
Bills problem
Just a word or two about a problem
Atmosphere
Drought
And nuclear
Warfare
Fire burning out the forest everywhere
Panic starting to sprout
No care more and more and more each year
Problems

MY DREAM

Sometimes I dream
Of being all
That Jah wants me to be
And of finding the lady
That will always
Be there for me
I dream of all the good things
In this world
For us to see
And my love ones free
The sky the sea
Help for the poor
Out of poverty
I dream of love so strong
That it would rid the earth
Of all its wrong
And right would be given
Total prosperity
That would last
Through total eternity
I dream of love
Created so well
It would spread
Throughout the world
Breaking all its spells
Even hold up
In the fires of hell
Even in heaven it grows
Swells

The only one relationship
Time won't tell
I dream love
That is so right
It will fill my days
With joy
The same in my nights
My favorite toy
And when i need it
Hold me so tight
Make me a king
And always do right
I will make her
My queen
I'll always do right
We will reign
And in love we give light
In Jah name we give praise
I dream the whole world would
Stop the fight!

MOON AND STARS

If I could catch a nova
I'll ride it into space
Take off in October
Like I was being chased
I would circle around the sun
So I can see its face
Because mercury
Is the smallest one
I'll fly by making haste
Venus orbits love and fun

Neighborly
I will embrace earth
I will just hit and run
And a hello to my race
Mars
I will pack my gun
War might be the case
Jupiter
Is the largest one
Going by there
I will keep my pace
Saturn
With the circle bun
I'll streak by
Without a trace
Uranus
I will land upon
And give to it my grace
Neptune
I will glide through
Its ocean
Like an astro
With no time to waste
Pluto
My voyage will be done
There I will state my case
I am a human being
On the run
From the planet
Jah gave my race
Home base

MIND TIME

Rooster crows
At working time
What he knows
to the rest
Is blind
Early bird
Out of the nest
Gets the e-z find
Cock a do
From the chess
Wake up caller
Is on the line
Dawn in the east
He crows
Same time in the west
A minute to the hour
Thinking mind
Rooster crows
Tells the time
What rooster knows
Every second is divine
Tic crock
Tic crock
Tic crock
Right on time

LOVE CONQUERS THE BEAST

The lion s out of the cage
And the trainer don't know where he is
He's broken out
In care of rage and seems to have just disappeared
Peace
He is out to wage
All war among us
Beware
Turn a new page
On the wrong doers
And the greedy one
Unfair

Cock your 12 gage
The lion is getting near
It is a shame
What he did to that cage
Wicked hearts will
Surely fear
Lion love
Is all in rage
You don't want him there
Your love is his daily wage
He is hunting love sincere
Out the cage
The trainer
Don't know where
Beware the lion

LOT

Babylon
Babylon
You're so wrong
Trying to bring
A good man down
Sent your clowns
Into their towns
Teaching the people
Your cold songs
Telling the people
The good news
Wrong
Bribing the people
Through the things
They long
Jiving the people
Into Babylon
Separating the people
Breaking their sound
Telling the people
The good man
Is wrong
Making the people
Town a Babylon
Good man good man
Don't turn around
The people
Babylon
Wrong

KEYLOCK

The truth is the key
To the lock
That will set you free
In the house
With peace and solidarity
With love and prosperity
With happiness and humanity
The truth is the key

The lies are the lock
To the door
Of the house
Between the hard place
And the rock
You won't hear
When goodness knocks
Put stumbling blocks
In your work
You will lose your respect
Around the block
The lie is the lock

HOLD DEM JAH

Run for your life
The dragon
Has been released
Babylon
Is his wife
They have came
To take away peace
And bring the whole world
To strife
Their son is called
The beast
And his tongue
Is a two edge knife
It is heat (guns)
He will increase
To destroy
The Holy One's life
Until all good on earth
Have cease
The prince of darkness
Is he whom must be stopped
Before she becomes
The dreadful
King of the beast?

GENESIS

Sister brother
It is written
For us to see
Remember back
In the garden
There was
A wicked tree
Put in there
To take our sight
And make us
Ungodly
Putting the right
Where wrong
Supposed to be
Making one think
They're in the fight
When you are the enemy
Getting wealthy
From poor family
Living under the influence
Of the wicked tree
Their life become
A low one
And a misery
And yours become
A high one
A fantasy
And the two is totaled
Blinded
By the same damn
Wicked tree

FISHER END

Like a virus
In your lines
Hit your screen
Knock you out
Blind
Web your sight up
blow it mind
Serious virus
On the line
Name is Irish
It's luck fine
But you are not
If it gets you
Into your vines
A furious virus
Get you from behind
Phishing virus
With net
Hook
Online
Deceiving babies
Before they grow
They're blinded
Preying on ladies
When feeling low
And crying
Stealing another identity
Like it is a treasure
You lost they find
A deadly, deadly virus
On our computer

Line
Catching our sight
I think
I thought my kids were safe online
Like a virus mind

FALLING ANGEL

You have lost your grace
Now you're here on earth
Segregating our race
Telling rich man
Poor man
Stay in your place
Black man white man
Judge by the face
Rat race
Taking our children away
And leaving not a trace
Got all the educated minds
On earth
Caught up in their own space
not knowing of what
They are looking for
Navigation wild goose chase
Sending billions
Up in the air
The poor are left to waste
The whole ghetto situation
Is crack cocaine and lace
You get hooked
With just a taste
How can there be
A happy-full
Homecoming
They can't even reach
The first base
No one gives
Like Jesus anymore

But for money
We suck up in haste
Two countries fighting
From two worlds apart
Is there really
Not enough space
Murderers of the prophets
We seek
But they never
Can be found
Quit! It is a cold case
Falling angels
All around me
When will they show their faces

COMING HOME

Sister, sister
Hang in there
Your man will be home soon
He might not
Bring back
A golden chair
Or even a silver spoon
He is a soldier
Fighting
No fear
For our country
Side by side
His armed platoon
Protecting our right
Our daily welfare
Around the clock
Morning through midnight
Evening and high noon
Laying their lives
Down
Twenty-four hours a day
Under the songs
Of the a.k. tones
Sister, sister
Your brothers
Will be home soon

BRUTE AGAINST THE BEAST

Trap in the boot
The gladiator
Truth
A lion by root
Lead a half million
Troops
Armed from the loot
A bomb
In the boot
The wilderness regiment
Mute
March for the truth
Winning battle after battle
But trapped in the boot
Armed from the loot
War on the brute
Cornered in the boot
Spartacus was the truth
Break your bonds with Rome
He just wanted
To go home
Lion by root
Trapped in the boot

BABY "ALLOWGIE"

Babylon cannot rule over us all together
He has divided us and now he rules
Together we are united with the creator
All separated we will never
See his light
We have been to the moon and back
Around the world and within its cracks
There is only One God and our condition states that fact
How did we get so divided?
Why hasn't technology taken us back?
Are we inventing separation?
Has our knowledge created world segregation?
Have all we've learned taken us out of reach of Jah congregation?

ALL MONEY

Does money
make it all right?
Does it even
Make us tight?
Make us see the light
Does money bring delight
Makes you want to fight?
Increases the fright
Or does it give you might
Does it make you polite?
Make you think
You are right
Do you keep it
Out of sight?
Or it shows on you
Bright?
Does it give you
Appetite?
Can you always chew
All you bite?
Makes you uptight
Does it take you
Through the night?
Does money put
Your love in flight?
Makes you hate despite?
Does money take you to the higher height up on a string like a kite?
What is this thing makes money so?
Does money write?

A HOLY EARTH

A good place
With everyone good
A good race
Ran the way it should
With no
Foreigner case
Only one neighborhood
With smiles
On every face
Loving and caring
The way that
Jah would
Zion
As home base
Together
We know we could
Create
A holy race
One big holy race
And forever
Live in its goods
Make earth
A holy place
One big holy neighborhood
In his grace

YOUR LAND MY LAND

The world is mine
And so, it is yours
We all together
Make up man kind
We all have flaws
But from Judah
There comes an old lion
That rules the whole earth
He roars
Takes down
All of earth's barriers
And make equal
Fair
All of earth's laws
He roars
Feed all of earth's hungry
And end
All of earth's wars
He roars
The world is mine
And so, it is yours
So, let us rebuild man kind
And live
For its cause
He roars

WHO KILLED OUR SON

Hey Mr. General Man
Do you know the soldiers that are marching behind you?
Now you have them marching straight
Every man have been sworn through
Are you sure every man swear heart is brave
True
And soldiers
Do you know
This general
Whom is leading you
Are you sure
That what he stands
And fighting for
Is right
True
And will he be there for you
When the fight
Is through
Or hiding out
At a distance
Telling you what to do
When fire breaks out
In the heart of war
Someone's bullet
Gets lodged into you
The madness of the war
You never know who

TIME CREEPS

The time is passing in a streak
The days are moving faster
Into weeks
Like in the days of the romans and the Greeks
When the prophets rise up and speak
Have mankind reached their peak
Our earth is getting weak

There is a hole in our sky
There the ozone leaks
We have forgotten about the paddle
That brought us
Up this creek

SERPENT

A mouth and a tail
Low side of the scale
The Jew
That hammered the nails
The snitch
That escaped the jail
The black
That is in the mail
The thirst
That tips over the pale
The rich
That bought the bail
The vision
Of the long red tails
The curse
And the summer hail
The cause
Of the vanishing whales
The truth
The lie
The holy grail
The whole damn world
Is up for sale
Garden snake
Your venom have not yet failed

SCARECROW IN THE GARDEN

Please don't
Drop the bomb
We will never recover
Its harm
It might seem like
We have
The whole planet charm
All the people in it
Eating
Out of our palms
But people take heed
To this silent alarm
This earth we live
Is the human race
Mom
And it is her children
We grow
On her farms
Eden will not survive
The venomous
Nuclear bomb

RISING KINGDOM

Tiny kingdom
But great
In numbers
When we try to stop them
Will they overcome us
Or maybe one day
Take the whole world
From us
They're growing so fast
On the land
We've been promised
How can we stop them?
Will there be hope for us
It seems
They have been
Doing their own thing
Since the very first day
They met us
Growing stronger
Minute by minute
They are catching up
To us

OUT OF ORDER

Standing on the corner
Taking a look
At the new world order
Families run by daughters
More faces
Crossing the border
Jail houses
Over run by brothers
Being bused
Just like the charter
Man of the house
Is the mother
Something must be
In the water
Food taste just like
Mortar
The holy ghost
Is the father
Something else
Is the other
It is a fairy tale
Like harry potter
My vision failed
Standing on the corner
Taking a look
At the new world order

MONKEY IN OUR SPACE

Monkey first in space
I wonder what
We learned?
Is he now
The leader of that race?
Should we be concerned?
Would he beat us
Into heaven,
And leave us
Here to burn?
I hope that's not the case
We all know of heaven
Bliss
It must be honestly earned
Are we behind them
In that chase?
And their place is
For what we yearn
Mankind
We must all make haste
Before the monkeys
Tables turn

TILL HE SAYS WELL DONE

It will be seen
In the rising of the sun
The sky will turn gray
As though
The end of time had come;
The righteous
Will be giving praises to Jah;
The wicked
Will be on the run,
This day will be a different kind of day
A different kind of heat will be felt,
In the rays of the sun, the angels of Zion
Will be blowing the horns;
In a Rasta man's song
Saying all you righteous people get up
Stand up, the good work has been done
The king of kings has returned to earth
He has captured the Babylon system
And have broken into pieces the enemy and his gun
Walk in peace
No need to run
He is the trinity
The almighty one
With all the lions of David
And the wisdom of king Solomon
Praise be his name
Unto the ends of this earth
For on this day
The truth will give birth
To this fire
That will make cold

The fury heat of the sun
It will not stop burning
Until the evil
Of this earth ends.
Well done.
Cooking. Well done.
I call him Jah
By his holy and righteous name
When he sets free his holy lions
All fake gods will leave the scenes
They will not be there to take
Anyone's blame
There will be left
No prophets
To take away your screams
If you are not running straight forward
With Haile Selassie I
By then you will be running straight backward
For the fury fire of flames

BROTHERS

Make us able
Lord
Keep us true and sane
Hold us stable
Lord
When negative waves
Rocks through our brain
Don't let us label
Lord
Color or creed
Faces eraser
When hearts are clean
Band of brothers
Sisters
Together like a cable
Lord
So that one can't be
Singled out
So low
Like Cain
Make us able
Lord
Help our love
Come down
Fertilize our gardens
Lord let it reign

LANDLORD

The landlord of the white house,
Your lease will only last
For four years
Just a few families get extensions
Some for the good work
Others for the fair work

Landlord, landlord
How many tenants have you cleared
That really showed us
They cared
From George to George
How many more
Before you
Paint your doors
Who will be the next family
To leave their prints
An echoes upon your floors?
Will they be for the poor?
I hope they come and leave peacefully
And not just try to even up scores
Landlord check their past history
Before you give them the golden keys to the locks
Of our white house doors

HUNGRY

World peace
Hunger will decease
All the freedom fighters
Must be freed
Release
So that the hate among us
Will not increase
But cease
We must stop feeding
The revelation beast
Cast out the bad tenant
In these last days
Of the Babylon lease
Burn their gates
And fences
Rain on their wicked feast
With world peace
Hunger will decease
And the clothing
We will wear
Will be that of
A golden fleece

HOT LINES

Hidden behind
Information hot line
Coming at you from the blind
Making sho'
You see the signs
If you're slow
Then ride the pine
Because it is
Designed
For the consciousness
Of your mind
That you know
It's one of a kind
Love lines
Rap lines
Social lines
History lines
Poetry lines
You will be fine
It will make you kind
Make you seek
You will be fine
You're not weak
Take your time
You're the meek
Information hot line
So unique

HIGH CLASS

Which class is high?
Rich class is low
Is it the money you got,
Or the things you show (borrowed)?
Who teaches it
And what skills
You need to know?
High class
What does it takes to pass?
How can i enroll to go?
Does the things you learn there last?
Guaranteed you won't be class low
The life with the greener grass
High up in the dough
In the hills
House made of glass
At a desk in room 44
Being tested
By the high class
Is it what you got
Cash or what you know?
The past
One million dollars
Or an a plus
Which will i pass?
Where will i go?
High or low class

MAN EATING BEAST

Low beam
High beam
From out of darkness
Came human being
Into the light
To drink from the stream
Of good and evil
And the fountains
In between
To eat from
A garden
Fruit grown fresh
Clean
Like Adam taught
His beloved sons
Abel and Cain
Don't let
The beast the field
The sin of the flesh
Sow seeds
In your heart your brain
Low beam
High beam
Let us share the gardens
With the beast of the field
Man should not kill or eat
That which came
From his own vain

LOVE AND LIBERTY

Love letter
To the statue
Of liberty
When I saw her
Something strong
Just took over me
Dear Libbie
I love you
I've toured your city
I know you're true
In central park
I will walk you through
Jersey to the Bronx
Want to make
The old
Brand new
On the Brooklyn bridge
Kiss away
Your blues
And on the Broadway streets
Make a wish
Shine our shoes
Harlem
We will meet
On a liberty rendezvous
Manhattan all dressed
Neat
Queen I love you
The apple of my eye
Sweet Lady of liberty
My boo Statue

LIONS

Is the end near?
A time when no one cares
Hate beginning to flare
Love don't mean sincere
The truth is in the rear
Disaster can't be compared

Something foul is in the air
Good vision cannot see clear
Religion have lost it flair
The cry have lost its tear
The crows have join the scare
Right and wrong is now a pair
And all fingers are pointed over there
Oh my dear
The lamb
Is no better than the bear
The end of sin
Is near

JAIL TALK

In my heart
There is only one love
My aim is pointed
In one direction
My destiny
To make peace
Into a human
Perfection
Release the innocent
Wrongly in correction
For the freedom
Of speech
And the hate system rejection
Stop taking away
The people connection
To jail
Less perfection
Without bail
For the liars
Free speech protection
In my heart
There is only one love
For truth
My aim is pointed
In one direction
Justice
With free words
And affection

GOLDEN BOW IN THE SKY

Silver arrows raining down
The angels are at war
The table have turned around
Putting an end to evil
At the places where it is found
Silver arrows raining down
Every country, every state, every city, every village, every town
There will be no escape from the evil thirst hound
His target is the heart
Where the wicked blood is found
His mission is to stop the wicked days that have been prolonged
So, when you feel the rain drop
Remember the great flood songs
All dem didn't drown
Suckers of blood have spread their evil back around
But silver arrows are raining down
Angels making once again Earth in to holy ground

GATE PLANTATION

I am
An island boy
Hilton head island
Raised among the plantation
Watching the rich
Behind the gates
Just smiling
In their life of segregation
While their stock and bonds
Go piling
Off their slave built population
In their fancy cars
Just styling
Mansions with the latest decoration
Rich children on the beaches
Wilding
Tourist from all around the nation
Big businesses on their phones
Just dialing
Talking about this celebration
On this little Hilton Head Island
What they didn't say
That its Partition
And we been here first
They have no relation
Now I, and I need
Emancipation

FINISH

They've got me
In a maze
So messed up
I'm amazed
So many different faze
Fraction
Full of phrase
Attention
In a daze
Dimension
Narrow ways
Intention
To make me craz-y
Slip me in a phase
Now don't think
That I'm a laz-y
I've got to change
Re-arrange
My life ways
Find me
In this maze
My straight path
To better days
My class
The one that pays
At last
I am amazed
Start

DOLLAR

Every living day
The cost of living
Keep on getting higher
People living
Day to day
Just making up
For lost
And dates
That have been expired
Bills are already being paid
One month late
And the cost of living
Is still getting higher
Life price is growing
At an alarming rate
Soon it will be
Only for the buyer

CAVE MAN

You made your home in the cave
Man
King of the beast
You was a brave
Man
Create the turning wheel
The road you pave
Man
Killing was your deal
Took not gave
Man
You loot and steal
And bad behave
Man
You lived like the dogs
And you never bathe
Man
Fed your family the hog
And that is unsaved
Man
Create the stumbling blocks that have enslave
Man
But you remember Noah the ark
He was the man whom awaited that big wave
Man
Rest in peace in your grave man
The whole place belongs to the roots
Of king Dave man

BROTHER AND I

Toe to toe
Just you and I bro on the go
Taking our lyrics to the show
Letting people know it is a better way to throw
Riddles and rhyme without using the
B's and N's
Throwing the signs of a positive flow
Easing the mind of the children
Let them grow until they find their way in life
They need us bro.
In this time you and I, toe to toe with positive lines
I and you must run the show
Send it through the grape vine
Bro.
Hey Babylon
You must go
Toe to toe
With me and my bro
Babylon.
Babylon, you must go
Low

BELOW

Mine eyes have seen
The ways of men
I don't like
What mind eyes see
Man-kind is hastily
Becoming a threat
To the sky
Land and sea
Our ways have got to take
Some changes
Before the new century
Or our eyes
Will see and end
But before that
There will be
Pain and misery
Misery
Like never before
Visions of a rising fire
Furiously
Burning blow
Waiting and watching
On all noun
Who is mark to go
Below

AMERICA

America the great country of many races
Divided into fifty-two states
The land where their lives grace
Together
To overcome hate
One land one love
Straight up into space
Red, white, and blue
Less empty plates
Every man choses
Votes his own faith
No trying mind is left to waste
Of whom he or she wishes to embrace
Every woman gets to choose her mate
And runs the race for leadership
That was once only a man's race
America the great
The country of many faces

A JESUS MAN

Am I a Christian?
Do you have the fear of the lord inside of you?
Do you have the care?
Would you have bled to death on a cross with Jesus,
With a belly full of gall?
Could you have stood tall, straight up
To the roman soldiers in faith,
Not with the sword like Peter or Paul
Could you have denied 30 pieces of silver
To give a kiss to the son of man?
Could you have been the one
To stop the A.C. clock?
There was no Christian in the B.C.
One Christian
For his whole 33 1/3 years
Can we really handle the conviction
Am I a Christian?
No!
And I know one only
The man whom is the son.
Are you a son of man?

A RIGHTER

It comes through the mind
And straight to the pencil
Then on the lines
Making it visible
To read over
In time
Changing the unagreeable
Perfectly kind
Words more meetable
In writing
There is no crying
Write what is considerable
To the old and the young
Write about trying
About the believable
The poor
Not the lying
Hate is retreatable
Through positive lines
Love can be
Cleavable
When it comes
To the mind
Straight to the pencil
Visible lines
Can some time blend
Read it over
A few times
The righter
Writes the lines

POSSIBILITY

Mission impossible
Making me over stand
Mission impossible
Reasoning with
A selfish man
Mission impossible
Teaching one
By demand
Mission impossible
Diamonds for free
Millions for sand
Mission impossible
An entire world
Playing the tone
One band
Mission impossible
Live your whole life
Without a helping hand
Mission impossible
Plant your family root
Without family land
Mission impossible
For the rich cup to over flow
Into the hungry empty pans
Mission impossible
To stop the ignorant of hate
Once the singer songs
Hits the fans
Mission impossible
To make peace
The human race

Without the whole body
Being a part of the plan
Mission impossible
To survive in the future
Without the wisdom
And leadership
Of king David's grand
Impossible

PEACE FULL

The prince is on the rise to win the peace
Is his surprise to stop the beast and his despise
Before he increase
Hate and lies and release
His genocide
Through the filth, deceit
He advertise the wicked ways
He socialize
It is never all that meets the eyes
But the prince of peace, He will sterilize, and save the least
He will fertilize and feed the least
There'll be no more cries
He will rule
Give free His prize
Through your school
The prince of peace
Will rise

OVER TALKING OVER

Just a conversation
About love and relation
Peace and education
Hope and motivation
Faith and inspiration
A simple conversation
About joy and happiness
Friendship and gladness
Neighbors and bliss
Honor and holiness
An easy conversation
About children and gardens
Rainbow and birds
All being pardon
And memories forgotten
A fresh conversation
About you and I
Brothers to the most high
Praying together
To the most high
Keepers of one another
To the most high
Protector of each other
To the most high
Playing together
To the most high
Respect one father
To the most high
Just Conversation

NOSE B-LEAD

Every time
You're on the scene
You just got
To get up high
Talking
Thinking about it
All the time
Can't ever
Just say goodbye
But E.Z. said
To the bill's money
When you go out to buy
Doing things
You've never done before
Smelling
Selling
Like telling
So damn much lies
Takes you
Makes you feel
So good
When up high
You feel
Your problems
Over
You can fly
The moneys gone
And the jones is on
It wakes
You fake your crying
Guiding you all wrong

One day your spirit
Will die
Freeze
Rudolph
The snow is a head
Your nose
Is all red
You're snorting away
Pies
Back to reality
Ask any question
The answer is always why?
If powder
Control your destiny
Then your love ones
You deny
And you are a follower
Noses in front
Being led down
Buying the high

NATIVE ISLAND RAPP

Surprise packet
Delivered
Unto I
On my
Back door step
Talking about
An island
With a very old
Bad rep
Everybody's business
Thrown down
On my mat
Right on my back step
12 plantations
Which the blacks
Do not
Except
Bias education
Where the blacks are being
Reject
Land taxation
Where blacks are being
Effect
Neighborhood separation
Where the blacks are being
Attack
The island segregation
Is keeping the blacks
In the back
Of the plantation
I read it

Out in the packet
Thrown on my back step
All about
How this little island
Kept a very bad rep
Plantations
All in the packet

MOVING OUT

Dreamy days
Wondering nights
Mornings of fright
An evening gull with gaze
Twenty-four hour feelings
Uptight
Seems we're living
A maze
So much confusion
Wars being fought
The whole situation
Is just a haze
Who is wrong
Who is right
Caught up
Is our own ways
Educated
But not bright
Some say
It is just a faze
Out of darkness
In to dreamy night
Lit with fire
Set to blaze
Morning of fright
And wondering days

MOON

Where have our prophets gone
Have the almighty god
Left us here all alone
Or is it that he just can't put
Up with our deceits and scorns
Or maybe there's
No one left on earth
For him to warn
Have we went too far?
With our
Microwaves
Internet
Space ships
And telephones
No one here
Speaks in tongue
Since the Apollo
Came down
Why is that Mr. Glen John
From the day you landed
Sound
Back upon this earth
The spirit of the prophet
Seems
To have been overthrown
I wonder
What chased the prophets away?
And to whence
They have gone
Technology came in style
And the truth
Went out style
I wonder what went wrong

MIND FLOATING

Mind floating
And mind adrift
Far away from port
High up on the water fall cliff
A captain-less boat
Sailing for just a whiff
The powerful remote control by the nose sniff
Sap of the wicked halt
Through the eyes of the needles
An awakening
Sleepy gift
A pill lower higher
Triple x coated
Ship off sail
Adrift
Mind floats
To the edge
Of reality cliff
Captain-less
Boat
Without a lift
Away from port
Mind afloat
And mind adrift
A stiff

STILL THE SAME

When the king rises on his way
To the throne to fulfill the holy mission
For what be have been born
Define the Solomonid Kingdom that have been lost
Considered gone
It was built to last forever
It will outlast the wicked scorn
Its treasures will be returned
From whence it has been pawned
Its land will be recovered
From whom
It has been loan
Its wisdom it eternity
It could never
Be brought back
A clone
Its powers is the trinity
And these days
Are about to dawn
Its people
Are only a few
But many shall be warned
It is nothing new
Biblical pictures
Have been drawn
The lion is coming through
Ethiopia is the horn
Still the same

MY WORDS

What can we do I do
For you Father with my pencil and mind
Is there something I can say?
Blind
To my brothers and sisters
Your children
That can help us in this time
Your world
Is changing every day
With all these new symptoms
But no one sees the signs
We have got to straighten all up
Get our earth back in line
Before we blow up this whole world up
Leaving
Only eight planets
Left in our system
Instead of nine
All of this space
There is only us
Let us save mankind
For our father
He is busy

IN THE WIND

Floating in the winds of the most high
Looking over my sins
From the most high
My soul is looking thin
I just want to cry
Lord
Where have I been
You know today
I'm trying
Lord
I follow the wrong men
You open
The doors to faith
My eyes
Now I have to say
Amen
Teach me to fly
You help me with my sins
Teach me no lie
Still my soul is looking
Thin
I just want to cry
I feel it
From within
All the wicked lies
In places
I have been
It is hard
To say goodbye
To my family and my friends
But now I've got to fly

Away from all these sins
Up, up
To the most high
Floating in the wind

I PRAY

As the first sight
Of the sun light
Ray
To bring forth the dusting
Of a brand-new day
First thing comes
To my mind
To call upon Jah
To guide my going out
And my coming in
And to protect
All of my words
Help me to be positive
In all
That I might say
Please move aside
All stumbling blocks
That have been put down
To block my way
Then I get down
On my knees
And pray
Oh Jah, Jah help us please
It is only
Your great name
I call upon when
I pray
I pray for all the sickness
To one day be cured
I pray
For all of our richness

One day recognize
Our poorness
I pray
All of my neighbors
To always be my friend
For peace
We work together
Until all wars
Have been seized
Be finish be stop be end
I pray
Special treatment
For all the old
Better than we treats
Our silver and gold
I pray
For all the new born children
Jah
Please make bless their souls
I pray
There be no more killing
All innocent set free
And for justice to judge
Equality
And not just
By ones color
Or by another
One pass history
I pray
For all my family
To always be together
To prepare our lives
And children
For both human changes

And change weather
I pray
For all the leaders
To lead the people with ca\re
To be
At their side
On a daily base
And not just only
On election year
I then pray
For myself
And start out on my way
Knowing my best work
Of the day have been done
It is Jah of whom
I pray
To keep my faith and health
The love I have for Jah
Is my most high
Valued wealth
I pray

GREAT DAY AHEAD

The great day
The day
When everyone says
Great is that day
And he
Whom pave the way
Is one
And all obey
All will work and play
As one love
Cry and pray
As one love
Built to stay
One true love
Is the holy way
Very great
Will be that day
When everyone all say
One love
The way Nesta say

FATHER'S WAY

My Father guideth me
I see his will be done
He leadeth I in such a way
As if I am his only son
Each morning
He gets me up
He give me work
He shows me how
To make an honest pay
He inspires my every move
My thoughts my deals my say
Unto him
I always
Kneel and pray
Every night
Before I lie down
I give thanks
For another day
I will break bread
With my brothers sisters and mothers
My father I will obey
My father loveth me
I love my father in the same way

EYE SEE

When will
This world wake up
Look within and see
It is written
In your Bible
Free
No one can say
It is a mystery
The Father is one
The Son is two
The Holy Spirit
Is number three
Jah
Put them all
In one good man
His name is Haile Selassie i
The light
Of this whole world
The might
Of the Holy Trinity
No man can sit upon his throne
No man can change
Jah history
The grandson of king Solomon
And the final root
To our father David family tree
Earth rightful ruler
The last ruler
This earth will ever see
Give thanks and praises
To I, and I Father

His holy name is
Selassie
King of Ethiopia
His imperial majesty
Conquering lion of the tribe of Judah
Crowned
By the lords and kings of this earth
On Nov. 30, 1930
Jah
Put them all
In one good man
And his name is Haile Selassie I
The first
Selah

BURDEN DOWN

He leadeth me to prayer everyday
And guideth me and cleareth my way
He provideth me
Light from his sons rays
He inspires me in every word
I might say it is His desire in me
For His eternal empire
I, and I pray
No eternal fire for me
His love will be my pay in Mt. Zion
High and free is where my burden wants to lay
Because he feedeth me with manna and with hay
My beast and my burden
I, and I will l never go astray
He leadeth me
He guideth me
He provideth for me
He inspires me
To pray everyday
He cleareth my way

OOO2

Positive you are
The good star
All right by far
The one whom
Brought us up to par
You fought dem law
You fought the war
You fought
All of our wrongs
You conquered what you saw
Your strength
Is still profound
Your love
Is still adored
Your work
Is still around
You have opened wide the door
You are the crown
You are the cure
Your heart
Crosses our grounds
Forever and forever more
One not now
But then
Was never before
Or after
How did we let him go?
Sorry

A11 EAR

Jah, Jah
I hear
What you are saying
Please help me to
Stay in
To you
I am praying
It's you
I'm obeying.
All night and all day in
You show me the way in
It's your love
That is paying
It's you that
Lies
Are betraying
I hear
What you're saying
Truly
I'm praying

LIGHT TO RIGHT

Dear Jah, Jah
I pray to you
To keep me
In your light
For all the things i do
Might sin
Between my night
And day
And for
In the future
From whence I've been
I have depended
On your might
Help me with my wrong
Help me to live right
So that I can be
Here long
To do your work
My plight
Because in this world
Of time and space
Our souls
Are all in spite
You are my only deity
My only guiding light
My might

ANDREW

Now I'm down to a Jackson
Still haven't seen no action
Financial state
A fraction
It's getting late
I'm lacking
The next bill date
Already attacking
I'm not straight
Nick-nacking
Anticipate
A backing
A kilo eighth
Start sacking
A M.M. nine straight packing
Back on the grind
Stop action
I'm out of line
One Jackson
Am I out of my mind
I'm macking a positive crime
No stacking
Blowing up minds
No packing
No key and no nine
No hacking
Gonna find mine
Action
But now I'm down here
Lacking
One last
Mr. Jackson Andrew

CONTROL OF ME

This stress is taking over me
The game is trying to take control of me
Brothers are dying trying to roll on me
Baby mama crying and she's calling me
This game is trying to take control of me
I am on the grind and that's bold of me
But I am just trying to feed my family
The triggers all spying
Players eyeing me
The streets all mine and it is calling me
I can see the signs
But it don't bother me
I'm not blind
But this Hennessy and this big nine
Gotta hold on me and this stress is trying
To take over me
My deals are flying
Taking control of me

DRAGON GAMES

Children of the dragon
Caught up
On the band wagon
Stumbling block
Now you're out there
Sagging
Not humble always bragging
About death
You're always bragging
Little lady love
Out there hagging
Sister girl thug
Out there nagging
Brother man bro
Out there swagging
Little Jonny O
On the block corners flagging
What happen to the prom
Everybody's going stagging
What happen to the games
Hop scotch, hide and seek
Red rover jumping rope
The simple games
Like tagging
All lost in the streets
Running with the dragon
Caught up
On the band wagon

FULL WHEELING

I've got to clear my wheel
Close down a deal
Break the sacred seal
Applying for appeal
Dem triggers done squeal
Not one real
I'll call in
The steel
A finish and done deal
I'm clearing my wheel
My baby done kneel
To some trigger she feels
My homies all teal
From playing
On their heels
They did not know
A player
Plays on his toe
I'm letting them go
I'm clearing my wheels
Closing all deals
Breaking
The sacred seal
They never really real
Applying for appeal?
Now they wanna squeal
Hater rat snitch eels
I'm clearing
All my wheels
If you fall off
The reel
Then your ass
Is seal
Clear wheels

BABY FAT

Find kind
Three figures dime
All in line
Baby's got back
Runs straight
Through my mind
All her chips stack
High
Damn she is fine
Addictive like crack
Damn
I want it all the time
The mother load
She is stack
I never go lack
When I'm on the grind
Baby's on the track
Taking
I mean
Tipping triggers blind
For when her thug gets back
Hit them with
A dance call wine
Get I'm caught up
In her act
Tell you baby's kind
I tell you baby's pack
It is part
Of that big behind
Tell you baby's fact
Three figures dime

All in line
Baby got my back
Baby blows
Minds
She is stack
She packs
She rules the tracks
Addictive like crack
Baby
Got my back

LET GO

Before I was
Number one
They had me
Two three or four
I didn't even know
They always let me go
Right after the show
I couldn't get a yo'
I even had dro
Tried
A little blow
But that shit didn't go
They thought
I was a ho
I would fall
When ballas blow
But I'm a hurricane
I keep my eyes
Low
Quiet storm
Cool and calm
Kicking in the door
I rock the stage
Floor
All the bridges
Burned
I'm letting y'all go
All you lovers
Come play learn
How to get that wo
You just be patient
Wait your turn

Yo'
Player play slow
Don't you haste it
No
Let it play
Hit it, rapp it
And you earn it
Now what you say
Shit
Number one
Two three or four
Out wit
They never let me go
I got them all
Smoking dro'
Letting them ballas go

ONE STRIKE

Man I just got
Out of the pen
I'm thinking about
Going at it again
I've went down
Twice
In this game
One more time
I will never be seen
On the scene
I should be trying
To keep it clean
Cuz'
I've got my mind
On selling that green
With two strikes
Caught with a nine
And I'm fresh green
Out the pen
Gotta catch
Up with my boys
Roll out with my friend
Gonna be a true player
In these streets corner
Once again
Down two times
Three time
The end
Wanna get up my grind
Don't know what's
Round the streets

Bends
Post up
On the corner
Just got done
Doing ten
And five before
Half of life
In the pen
And I'm thinking
Slinging
On this town again
Catch one time
Clocks out
On my game
It's locked
In my mind
Grind once again
I'm thinking
Vision green
In the back of my mind
Slip up
One more time
I never will be seen
On the scene
The life of confine
Grind
Just got out
The pen
I'm thinking

R.A.P. POET

My life is poetry
My future has
Approached me
Tells me to write
Poetry
Just let my faith
Coach me
Love and grace
Will tote me
Across the place
Float me
Poetic lace
Will coat me
All the races
Support me
Making haste
Promote me
In this chase
With poetry
If i waste
Demote me
Win or lose
Deport me
To Afrika
They will
Fort me
Support me

SHOTS CALLING

How can you live
Your life so high
Balling on misery?
How can you stack
Your flow's so high
Balling on misery?
How can you watch
Poor young mothers cry
Balling on misery?
How can you walk
The streets so fly
Balling on misery?
How can you watch
Those precious babies die
Balling on misery?
How can your heart be
So cold, so dry?
Balling on misery?
How can you slice up the poor
Getting your pie
Balling on misery?
Taking every penny
Leaving it ghetto dry
Balling on misery?
How can you expect
To prosper
When you are
Selling up lies,
Balling on misery?
How can you expect
Future free

When it is freedom
You take
From them whom tries,
Balling on misery?
You take their goods
Bring in fear
And in you affairs
The truth about you
Denied
Balling on misery?
How can you brag
About guns and keys,
Head hung up
In the sky,
Balling on misery?
My people your people
Time to eye-dentify
Balling on misery?

APPROACH

My first approach
First class coach
Sunset on the back-screen porch
Miami port luxurious boat
Tied up at my Miami Fort
When we float just for sport
In a corner that is remote
Bermuda Triangle
You, Love and I
Rocking the big boat
My second approach
Hands around the waist
Tongue down the throat
An extra feeling for the chase
And then we begin to float
The leather meets the lace
I reach for the remote
Turning you on channel after channel
All the way back
To the port
My last approach
Back to the fort
Tying you down
With a sweet slow
Love song
On my own play ground
Baby girl, you can't go wrong
I'm the biggest fish
Catching in the seaport town
No approach

BELOW LEVEL

When I drive
Through the city
And I see so many people
Living under
The lines of poverty
And just
Above the lines of hell
I see
One square mile
Of buildings and streets
With more cars and concrete than there is grass and trees
A most dreadful place for gods people to be
Trapped on an oasis and ignored
By the rest of the country
With no fresh water
No fresh air
And no help out of misery
That increase everyday
By police brutality
No sun comes in by day
And no moon comes out
At night
No stars to guide their way
The street corner offers
Their only light
More families than there are jobs
Some fall into the trap
Start to push
Rob
Living on the lines
Of hell you see

Everyone is a stranger
To the other
In the city
The codes are survival
And the ways
Is without pity
Under the lines of poverty
Because there
Is just above
The lines of hell you see
Housing in building
That are old and raggedy?
Why should it be the same
In the neighborhood
Elementary
The only brand new building
In the inner city
Is the police station
And the penitentiary.
When i drive through the city,
It grieves my heart to see
The condition of the people
Living under the lines of poverty.
It is like living
Above the lines of hell, you see.

BLING BLUE

South beach baby
It is the place to be
Mouse creep baby
Reservation by the sea
Just you baby
And the other
Me
Dream true baby
Fairy tale fantasy
Sky blue baby
And the water is to
Clubs hot baby
And the shopping is new
The scene is cold baby
Players and their whole crew
Platinum and gold baby
Big ballas rolling through
When we stroll baby
All eyes will roll on you
When they fold baby
We're going to split
The street in two
Diamond so old baby
The color have turned blue
Beats hitting bold baby
Breaking off the trunk screw
The south beach bowl baby
Washed up on the shore
Who
Me and you
Doing how we

Know to do
Mouse creep baby
Reservation by the sea
South beach baby
Dream come true
Pack the blue
Diamonds

BREAK AT DAY

The sun gives us light
And heat
The moon reflects
The fright
And cold be the city streets
The workers of nine to five
Go home
To rest and sleep
The players
The jokers the jive
Comes out and starts
To creep
Hustlers murderers ballers and pimps
Taking control
Of the whole damn street
Open up shop
Blowing up
Hot like the blimp
Thug territory
No place for a wimp
When the sun goes down
The streets changes in law
The good can't be found
The armies of darkness
Comes out
Make war
Triggers be creeping
With them A.K.'S
In their cars
The wo's
The robbers the gambler

The theft
Take over the alleys
Leaving behind them
Pain and grief
The junkies the addict
The crack heads the freak
They roam
The dark places
And prey upon the weak
The haters
The use to be frauds
The snitch
Stands in the light
On the side streets
Spelling you out
Like a witch
The cops the D.E.A., FEDS, C.I.A
They're all in the game
But play a different way
Trying to catch a trigger
As he plays
Through the night
Because he knows
A hustlers work is done
When he sees
The break of day

COMING THROUGH

Can't be
In no jail
I tried to stop
But I did fail
Hit the curb
And took some mail
Hit the hood
And the triggers them hail
But Mama
Just shout and wail
Her face
Was long and pale
Baby boy is going back to jail
Mama say
This shit is getting stale
Three strikes
And my ship has sailed
I can't stop
I've got three bails
The law arms are long
Like Kevin McCales
And I've already had
Three sales
Lord please don't let this Chevy fail
Coming through!

DEVOTION

On the beach
With my sweet lady
Enjoying the heat
The water is wavy
Miami heat
And the girls
Gone crazy
Surfing the beat
Smoking that hazy all in the street
But they don't phase me
Remembering ***Freak Meek***
I met my baby, the queen of the week
Now my flower of May day
When she hits the street
You won't ever forget
Memorial Day
In your memory
She moves in a motion
With pride and devotion
She's got that love potion
Don't need no tan lotion
She plays with emotion
Give your eye a beauty promotion
Makes you want to die
The Atlantic ocean on the south beach
Don't lose your devotion
Ladies and gentlemen
Slow motion

FOR THE GHETTO

How can we make things right?
Why can't we give them free light Down in the ghetto?
Where hope always stays out of sight and no hope keeps you on lock down tight
How can we make thing right??
Can you give them water for free down in the ghetto?
Where there is so much misery and not enough time
Spent being happy
How can we make thing right?
Rent for free down there in the ghetto
Where the houses are so old
Summer hot and winter cold
Nothing works but everything is sold
The rats and roaches are out of control
How can we make it right?
Can we give then transportation for free down in the ghetto?
Where the highway robbery is called the city taxi?
And city buses don't include the ghetto
As part of the city
Can we give pity

HIGH RAP

Hip hop
How you do
Yes I'm moving
On your crew
Non-stop
Straight on through
Rock pop
Cash in too
Hits drop
One and two
Close shop
Open new
Call the cop
Coded blue
On the top
Resting you
Until you stop
Coming through
Give it up
That won't do
Rap high

KEEP RUNNING

Boy you better run
Look what you done, done?
Bad boy you better run
Now you're playing
With that gun
Bad boy you better run
I'm talking to you son
Bad boy you better run
A bad rude mon
Bad boy you better run
Playing bloody
Trick for fun
Bad boy you better run
A wicked throne
You sit upon
Bad boy you better run
Your right is wrong
Your faith is none
Bad boy you better run
When all is gone
You will have no one
Bad boy you better run
No man can be
His own honey bun
Bad boy you better run
That is in the keys Florida
That is in London
Bad boy you better run
Down to your knees
And boy don't run

ON THE RUN

I'm on the run
From my life
You see
I've messed up everything
Twice
No turning back
Nothing left
To sacrifice
My girl done left me
Said I can't afford rice
My homies don't hang
They say I smells like mice
My boos don't call
They say I'm cold as ice
Gamblers don't gamble me
They say I fix the dice
Players don't play me
Say I talk to vice
The kids don't holla on me
They say that I'm not nice
My main chick is dogging me
Treats me like
I have lice
My situation done got stale
It's in the air
I've got to pay the price
I can't sleep day or night
My life is a poltergeist
Now I'm on the run
Running to save my life
I have messed up everything

I've lost
Everything
More than twice
And there's no turning back
Nothing to sacrifice
The only thing I have left
Is my next stop, Jesus Christ

OVER MY TRON

I checked her heart out
For my love
Come to find out
My love was gone.
Now my heart is broken
And I'm crying
Over my potron
I knew something was wrong
I sensed it
Through the phone
When I said my favorite lines
That shit didn't turn her on
Now I'm stooled up
In the club
Crying over my portion
Hearing these voices
Telling me
The love is gone
I'm telling myself it's wrong
Shit won't leave me alone
Now I'm at this bridge
Call scorn
Crying over my potron
When me and her
Was making love
She always cry and moan
Now it seems as though
She don't even feel my bone
Is my shit getting smaller,
Or maybe her shit
Is grown?

Now I'm over here
At my homeboy house
Crying over his portion
Every time I go by now
That girl is never home
Always finding reasons
For us not to be alone
When she says
She loves me
Her voice changes in two tones
Now I'm on a busy highway
Swerving
Crying over my porton
I had to moved out
Packing
I had to move on
Nothing here to stay for
I saw
The love was gone
I saw her a year later
She was macking
A dirty blonde
And I finally found out
Then
Where our love went wrong
My baby was on potron

SET UP

Down in the jail
All filled up
With young black male
Being black mailed
In there for
A sale
Going down
At an alarming scale
For coke crack smoke bails
By snitches
Who's telling tall tales
For men the color pink and paled
Helping to put them
Into extinction
Just like they did
The great whale
One day your bias plan
Is going to fail
And the prison train line
Is going to derail
And the rock are going to
Fall back
On your mail
Just like hail
But hold on tight
You are the holy grail
Young black male

SHOPPING MALL

New number baby
That is why I didn't call
New baby, I got it from the south side mall
I heard about you baby
There is a lot
Of talk in the hall
I read about you baby
It's written
All over the walls
I cared about you baby
Now shit's
All over the stall
I spared nothing baby
You never gave it all
I shared everything baby
You was my baby doll
I gave you stability honey
But I see you wanted only to ball
Look what you have done to me sweetie
Almost made me fall
Feeling clowned and misery
So I went down to the shopping mall
Step in the rest room
And what did I see
Your games written
All over the walls
Turn around and luckily
Bump into
A brand new baby doll
Got her numbers
Change mind
That is why I didn't call
New numbers baby
I got it from the south side mall

THE GIFT

How will I ever come back from this
How will I attack my poor life
Dis-
How will I restore my soul my bliss
I've got to reach one on the top list
Step right up, take a risk
Get back all things, I need I miss
Get this place
Eating from my fist
How will I ever
Come back from this
MTV
A brand new dis
B. Movie
Restore my bliss
Three CDs
On the top hit list
DVD no heed
Taking a risk
Gift and greed
The places I miss
Get all my needs
Platinum
Laid across the fist
I will succeed
On the top ten list
Don't have to plead
I got it
Out my gift
How will I ever
Come back from this

THREE LOOK

When I first saw the light
I can't remember the night
Skeed up in the club
Taking on my buzz
And there I was
In the middle of my grove
When this pretty lady
Cross my sight
What first came to my mind
She's a nice fine looking lady
But she was all right
Then I took a second look
And though I saw a light
There she was
Dark lovely beautiful and fine
Hit my mind
Shining neon bright
Everything put together right
A+ and #10 equals her
Figure is wrapped tight
Then I took a third look
I know I saw the light
Walked right over to her
Ask her how is your night
Then she started saying
The things that I had liked
Then I started noticing
She was a lady
But not of the night
Fine and polite
She chilled

With me tight
Made me feel the light
Gave me that number
Made my whole
Damn night
I made the call
Now she is my might
She's My genuine delight
Three looks I saw the light

THE ANT

Swift
Like the cheetah
Silent like the lamb
Deadly as a cobra
The wrath of UNCLE SAM
A gentleman but a soldier
Basically trained
To drill
Through and out the jam
Willing to be kill to live
A warrior mind
Stays on the front line
Forward and behind
Above the enemy dying
Seeking and destroying
When the general give the signs
Left right left right
Swift
Silence
And deadly all the time
U.S.M.C
One of a kind

OH HAPPY DAY

Happy birthday
I hope today
Things go your way
I hope today

Will be ok
It is your day
You should
Have your say
Wish and pray
Be happy and gay
Have it your way
It's your birthday
Hip-hip, he rays
Hip-hip, her rays
You were born
This day
Happy birthday
Your day

BANNER

We honor and salute
Our beautiful nation flag
Like a three piece suit
Red white and blue
I Braggs over Fifty States
And two under this tailor made
Ragg our country value
Our pride with in
The American peace
Flagg upon every pole
There rides a man
That united many
Under one
Red white and blue
Flagg
I Bragg

THE FRONT LINE

In memory
Of all soldiers
Whom fought
For peace and right
Who stands up
Against the odds of life
And gave it
In a worthy fight
Into darkness they went
Against dishonor and hate
And march bravely
In to the light
Warriors they were
Without fear or fright
I salute you all
Your courage shines bright
You are from god
You are his knights
We remember
You all
Your person your fight
We wish you all
A hero's good night
Soldiers sleep tight

MAGICAL

I give thanks
For the day
Thanksgiving
A day so unique
So caring so loving
The only single day
Of our whole year
That the living
Looks out
For the living
When families get together
To give thanks
For what they have
Been given
It seems this day
Everyone gets fed
Regardless
Of how they're living
Giving
For what they have been given
The living forgiving
To the living
Earth loving

A RACE LIKE ME

Take it gracefully
It is my time
There are many ways
For me
To bring my rhyme
It was made for me
It is in my signs
There is no lace
In me
Tough and kind
Not E.Z.
Facing me
I'm not blind
The future
Is chasing me
And fames
Right behind
Jah embracing me
Praying
All the time
Taking it gracefully
In my lines
Jah
Jah
Have space for me
You know
Dear Jah
I'm trying
No home base for me
Peace
Is no where

To be define
Here
I'm loving you gracefully
Holy place for me

PROFIT

Oh how precious
A gift to me
One with light
To help me see
For the good I write
And for him
I will be
Always in the fight
Against human misery
Trying to make right
What went wrong
History
Oh how precious
How priceless
This gift I have received
I will use it
To send a message
But never will I deceive
Because this gift
Is a passage
To what I truly believe
I will never
Take advantage
It is for love
That my heart grieves
My gift my light
I write
And my words
I hope will cleave

TUFF GONG

Bob Marley
Was a guitar playing man.
He brought a message
To the world
Through his reggae playing band.
He said
For all of us together
Get up and stand
Afrika unite
From afar
People of this land
Before we got
Caught and bought
Brought
Into the Babylon land
Exodus
Freedom fighters
We must demand
Buffalo soldiers
Was the keys
To the civil war stand
Redemption song
One love to all fans
The rebel music singer
Brought back memory
Of our old Holy Grand
He said
Haile Selassie I
Is
Earth rightful ruler
To this he under and over stand
The harp playing man
Marley

THE SAMPLES

Example
Example shown
Example taken
From the unknown
The truth is awaken
Human not clone
It is what love be making
A child is born
And Babylon is shaken
Remembering the horn
And where Sheba was taken
Now he's grown
And the whole world
Is faking
Judah stands alone
The lions have awaken
No more samples
It's the real thing
Awaken

SWEAR IN

All that praying
Is paying
I heard
What the Father was saying
And I
Was faithfully obeying
Because
He is
My only
Love way in
My reason always
To stay in
Night out and day in
The others are fading
To right
They won't swear in
They all are straying
Do wrong
They are saying
True wrong
They're obeying
And the whole
World is paying
Swearing

BLIND POOR

Lord have mercy on me
You know a poor trigger can't see
Brought up in a cold city
Ghetto life lives
Poverty never known
But misery
Lord have mercy on me
Caught up in
This game you see
Looking for the fame in me
While every body's
Blaming me
Baby mamas claiming me
Lord have patience with me
It came from overseas
Apart of the ghetto industry
Get paid
Selling pounds and keys
Ball on misery
Self-making
Wild and free
Lord have mercy on me
I thank you Lord
For all the good in me
Lord please
Have mercy on me

BLOCK SOLDIER

Around ten years old
With thuging on the mind
Watching every thing
The thugs do
On the grind
From the corner of their eyes
Sucking up every word
Every sign open ear
Developing
Their own lines
On every scene
On every block
Just waiting, watching
For that time
Blinded by the shine
Their little beady-eyes
Taking in everything
Like undercover spies
Ask
Did you see anything?
You know they're going to lie
Learning on the streets
In the streets
You talk you die
Block soldiers
Don't cry
Hanging on the corner
Watching everything go by
Skipping school
And rolling dice
Jacking cars

And getting high
Won't hear
A good thing
Not even their mother's cry
Their minds
Are on the corners
Hoping
Time flies
Gathering all
They need to know
To get a piece of
Street pie
Because
If you're gonna be a player
Stay fly
Your first education
Is to pass
Block highs

CITY FLOWERS

Girls strolling through the hood
Hair all done
Make up real good
With nail and toes
Matching their clothes
Looking like
A sweet flower thang
Every thang glows
Players around the block
Drown until the sight is gone
Fine as can be
In the inner city
Every shade

Every tone
Brown chocolate
Black beauties
Yellow jackets
Red bone
Strolling through the hood
Waiting on the phone
Looking real good
Some with friends
Some alone
The hood beauty
Ghetto born
Inner city
Home grown
Nothing finer
Homes
Then a hood grown girl
Charms
When she's in the zone

CRACK HOUSE

No Kool-Aid in the house
Not enough for a mouse
No ketchup in the house
Not enough for a mouse
No cereal in the house
Not enough for a mouse
No sugar in the house
Not enough for a mouse
No tooth paste in the house

Not enough for a mouse
No toilet paper in the house
Not enough for a mouse
No light in the house
Not enough for a mouse
I wonder who lives
In this house?
The three blind mouse
What do you call this
House?

ONE BEING

If I can just get rid of dem fools
Out the game
Keep talking up my name
Making up a scheme
Trying to split
My team
Playing with my dream
Delaying on my fame
Who's the one
To blame
Try to blow
Out my flame
Haters
So damn lame
The wild
Cannot be tame
My style
Have no shame
You and I
Not the same
But we share
A water stream
Both human beings
Share the cows cream
Let us not be fools
Playing
Old human games
We all are equal here
In this world
We dream
He didn't create
A man
Over another supreme

PAROLE AGAIN

Up in the hole
Again
Back on the stroll
Again
Getting real bold
Again
Back out control
Again
Out on the roll
Again
Blinging that gold
Again
Shipment is sold
Again
A ¼ mill fold
Again
Taking big toll
Again
Breaking that mold
Again
Trigger
Getting cold
Again
Game getting old
Again
Parole

SEVEN MOST

The seven most talented
Features in the streets

Number one is the hustler
He hustles every thing
And every one he meets
From head to feet
Got what you needs
He's got highs he's got lows
Even known to hustle meat
When you have been done wrong
And you're feeling the cold
He is your man
He hustles heat

Second is the pimp
Ho's he knows
Because he is a temp
He pimps the ladies
Whom have desperate needs
He attracts the others
With the ability
To sense greed
Some he gets
Have just lost their way
And need someone else to lead

Number three is the hooker
The looker
Of the looker
This job is the oldest

The first damn pro.
Pro. means the best
She sells her body
And do whatever to impress
Because getting that money
Is her mission
A nightly quest

Number four is the balla
Total shot calla
Now his job is the hardest
He has got to be
The smartest
He deals with big weight
Big money all the time
Packing big heat
And keeps
The whole damn block in line

Number five is the stripper
Temper of the tipper
Who's first love is always
The man
Whom is the big sipper
But what she's really
Looking for
The man
Who's money can equip her

Number six is the player
High roller woman layer
He knows the whole street
And everything
On and in it

Drives bad cars
Play bad girls
Do whatever it takes
To win it
Most players been in the game
For a minute
They rule the street games
The street games
Players plays invented it

Number seven is the gambler
Your money
His stamina
He make bets on everything
He never stops
Rather lose or win
His money watch
His diamond ring
He bets the numbers
It's an everyday thing
And at the track
A dog calls king
He rolls the crap
From seven to eleven
Then play poker
Until the morning springs rapper
Most of them are ex-gambler players strippers
Balla pimp hooker hustler
Some call trappers
From the project to the stages
Telling the hoods stories
Now making honest wages

SOFT PAIN

The rain fell soft
On my roof last night
I woke up with a cough
From that smoke
Last night
The heat is in the loft
From the hit
Last night
My trigger took off
With a mitt
Last night
I belittle
Like a dwarf
Got out wit
Last night
But I'm not playing soft
I'm lit
Fit to night
Lit up on the shit
Makes me cough
On patron patrol
Tonight
The heat
Is out the loft
I'm on the street
To night
Gonna take'em off
He'll be gone
Tonight
Put the heat
Back in the loft
It's gonna rain

Tonight
I'll go to bed
With that cough
Feel no pain
Tonight
On the roof
The rain fall soft
Down in the game
Tonight

THE DREAM NITEMARE

This is really a nightmare
That turned into a dream
My life was going nowhere
My price was looking lame
Took a walk to catch some air
Gotta change my target or my aim
And I stumbled over this broken lamp
I picked it up
And I heard someone call my name
Took it home cleaned it off
That night I had this dream
I dream rap
I lit the lamp
And a genie came
I dream rap
With all the fortune
And the fame
From the bottom of the keys
To the top of Boston, Maine
I dream rap
San Francisco, New Orleans
Mexico City, Jamaica, Queens
Afrika, Australia, straight, through Spain
I dream rap
Being king of the stages
Selling show out all over the map
Hawaii Canada, Italy, Iraq
Flying to the east
And sell the Jap's rap
I dream rap

Of living the kool life
All the styles and the hap
Hitting the clubs at night
With girls that dance in your lap
Dreaming rap
Of hanging out with the trap
One hundred entourage
And every trigger strap
Cold thugs from the streets
From busting the cap
One word or a signal
And every fucking trigger snap
Sealed tight like a blanket
Under cover in the gap
This is really a nightmare
That turned into a dream
I dream rap

THE WHOLE LOAD

You haven't house me
You haven't fed me
You haven't head me
You haven't read me
Now what is that
You just said to me
You want money
Just for free
Baby how much things
Have you done for me

Gave me a little bit
Of your sexy
Then tell me
You love me
Now i support the whole family
I know my a's and c's
I can count my i's and 3's
What's the amount
A fantasy
You don't even know me
House me
Feed me
Head me
Maybe you didn't read me
They already told me baby
That you are very heavy

TYPHOON

A soft rain
Started falling around noon
Cooling the pains
Of the hot sun
That looms above
The clouds
Waiting for an opening
But for now
It's a soft rain
Covering up
The rays
And filling the drains
Softly
Watering the scene
Quietly coming down
In individual grain
Each in it own lane
Hitting one by one
Upon the surface
Of the lake and stream
Tiny waves
Of the soft rain
Falling around noon
Cools the pain
Of the hot sun
Looms
The gentle typhoon

YOU'RE MY LADY

You're sweet
You're kind
You're funny
You're fine
You're neat
You're time
My mind
My vine
My line
My grind
My shine
Lady sign
Lady lion
Lady Zion
Lady divine

YOU BREEZE IT

When love
Is in the air
It carries every where
From ear to ear
You stare
Your heart beat
Feels the fear
Flare
You mind thinks
Thoughts of care
Your body wants
Just to be near
The one that makes
Your pair
There is nothing
You won't share
I love you
Is all you hear
There's no blue
In you
My dear
True, true, true
Sincere
You breeze it
It's in the air

WISHES

Roses and kisses
For you
All night
Memories and wishes
Of holding you
So tight
Time spent
Time misses
When you are away
Can't wait for the night
Flowers wine
Love song disc
Low burning fire
The setting
Put right
R Kelly, Barry White
Songs of bliss
The top ten lists
A time of ecstasy
Burning delight
Fruit flavored lips
Warm soft
Jelly like
Hyper genic kisses
By candle light
In our birthday suits
Lay down
Make wishes
All night
Giving you love
Until the sun shows

Bright
For the garden
Of roses and kisses
For you
Love wishes

WELL DONE

It is over baby
Well done
My heart has found
You're not the one
Too much drama
Jump the gun
Baby's mama
Bad ass son
Not the one
I've got to run
It's been fun
You will always be
My hun,
But baby girl
I'm not the one
You're not my pearl
I'm not your sun
In another world
We could be one
But not in this world
I've got to run

US

You have been
So good to me
As if thou
You've given yourself
To me
You try hard
All the time for me
You keep yourself
Looking fine for me
You're patient
And you're kind to me
Keep everything straight
In line for me
When we make love
You grinds for me
Always smoke
That sweet pine with me
Where ever I
chose
She dines with me
Her inspiration
Is one of a kind for me
Baby
Until the end comes to time
Of me
Little things you do
The affects you put.
Thought
Keeps love shining
Brand new
Away from the daisy of the blue

To you my dear
I will always be true
My love will be there
Always there with you
For you

TWO LIVES OR ONE

Two lives
Come together
Making one
Husband and wife
Two spirits
Join together
Having fun
Two hearts
Growing together
Under love's sun
Two bodies
Live together
Conjunction
Two minds
Thinking together
As if one
Time spent together
Til' life is done

TOO MUCH

I'm leaving you baby
You lies too much
Leaving you baby
You get high too much
Leaving you baby
For money
You cry too much
Leaving you baby
For love
You deny too much
Leaving you baby
Because you spy too much
Leaving you baby
You never try too much
Leaving you baby
You say
Goodbye too much
Leaving you baby
Our problems
Multiply too much
Leaving you baby
You're never
Satisfied enough
Leaving you baby
Your pockets
Dry too much
I'm leaving you baby
And you know why
Too much

TIME OUT

Your phone ringing off the hook
The whole of the night
Time out
The smell of fish
Scents in this house
Fright
Something just
Is not right
Times out
Frowns all day
All night uptight
Time out
Poetry and romance
I write is now fuss
Broken dreams and fights
Time out
Once unsaid
But still sure
Is now unsaid but might
Times
Baby
Have our good love reached
The failing height
Time
Have our once rainbow love faded to white
Time out
I feel darkness taking our space
In spite
Time out
In places
Where there

Should be only light
Destroying colors
That was once so bright
Time
Now I right the words
I did not want to write
Time out
Goodbye nite

THE THREE DIMENSION

Love for Jah
Love for self
Love for everyone else
The three dimensions
Of love
Should stretch the width
Of the world
Reach the height
Of the sun
And its length
Should go on for ever and ever
For all
The same
As for one
Love is a complete
Dimension

THE QUEEN AND I

Moving high up on top the bridge
Staying fly
Walking the ridge
A serious guy
No strap no gizz
Staying high
On me and my queen Liz
Elizabeth that is
The fairy queen of the wiz
Keeping clean in this bizz
Watching out for
The Miss and Ms.
Trying to tell me
All their fizz
Just like them witches
On the wiz
Oz that is
They must be diz
Flying around
Selling their bizz
Not me and Liz
Queen that is
We don't listen
To fizz
We just mission
Handle our biz
No superstition
On top of the bridge
Staying fly
Satisfied
My queen and I

Walking on the ridge
A serious guy
Staying high
On me and my queen
Liz
Elizabeth that is

FALLING ANGELS

Who knows
When the heart falls
And the angel calls
And you're backed up
Against the wall
You're in love
When the order is tall
And you're in the mall
And all you can think of
Is your baby doll
You're in love
When you drop
The baller
Now
Kissing in the hall
Giving her your all
You're in love
When you hear your inner call
You temperature goes up
And your pressure goes down
You're hanging low
And walking tall
You're in love
That is when
You call St. Paul
You know when
The angel call

THE BEAUTIFUL HUNTER

She is a tiger
With an angel smile
Hidden behind
Her perfect lady style
Stripes and fangs
A creature of the wild
In the night she
Hunts and prowl
Her beauty is bright
Hypocrite
Is her smile
Give you love frights
Of being stork
In the wild
She being your wonder light
To danger
With her smile
Lock you in her bite
Add you to
To dear john pile
She is a lady
In plain sight
But tiger roaring wild
Gentle and polite
A tiger is her style
A beauty in delight
A most venomous beautiful smile
She is a tiger with an angel smile
Hidden behind
Her perfect lady style
Drives the rabbits wild

SEALED AND CLOSE

So I am yours and you are mine
We two have chose
To go divine
Overlook the scares
The crows and focus
On yours and mine
As trust grows and secrets find
Love flow and special times
Always shows when words are kind
It opens noses to the beautiful scents
Passion signs like fresh cut roses
Dinner with wine highs and lows
Love sensation only you and I know
Yours and mine and future poses
of yours and mine
Sealed and close

SEARCHING

Searching for love
In every eye
I look
All emotions and moves
I check
All figures
I observe
Voices
I feel vibrations
Searching
In the night I wonder
If I'll ever find true
And love
In the day time
Eye see everything
Some by sight
Some by sense
But still
I gets no contact
Where is she?
Is there no one there
Am I alone
In my search
In vain
If not let me see
Let me see
Myself again
In my search
To find
The true love
Of mine

PURE TO PURE

Your heart is pure
In your eyes
I know
Your touch
Fills me so
Your love
Won't let me go
You are my high
It always show
My pacify
When I'm feeling low
On rainy days
You are my bow
Your loving rays
Just makes me glow
Eye to eye
Toe to toe
You are my babe
I am your booh
My arms are able
My heart is pure
I love you so
Pure to pure

PRICELESS

It is said
A good friend
Will last forever
And forever good friends
Will be true
It is very E.Z.
To be your good friend
Because I see
So much good in you
You make me feel happy
One
I like being with you
Two
And you're kindness to me
Three
Comes always free
But always brand new
Night or day
Little rest or none
For I
You always come through
I love you
I will tell no lies
For your friendship
I truly value
There is not much
I won't do
Stay nice baby
Stay kind sweetie
Everything
I feel is fine
Just like you

ONE LIGHT

Now
From the heart
To you I will
Tell and show
How much I really care
And everything
You needs to know
I think we have started
A fire
Getting too hot
For us to let go
It seems
We have been together
Lovers
In a time before
Until we find our destiny
Let us keep it
Burning on the low
We must keep on trying
To make more bright
This light
And let what's inside
Flow and grow
Your light
My light
Together
It is one sight
In time for us
It will glow
On

MISSION

Where, where are you baby?
Everywhere we go
You just disappear
I don't even know
Why
You think I don't care
I have tell
I have show
I will always
Be right here
In the E.Z.
High tide
In the hard times
Tides low
This love
I truly fear
And I dear
Not let go
So baby
Reappear
And let us
Repair it real slow
We are
A single pair
And dear
Only one way
We can grow
In love
Pairs

MAN TO MAN

Talk with her
Tender
Like a lady
Help her understand
Let her know
She is your baby
Kisses on her hands
Never tell her maybe
Maybe is not a plan
Always make sure
You say we
And show her
Who is the man
Give her love
Ecstasy
Whenever it is
In demand
Let her be
What she needs to be
Loving free
Be her number one fan
Her fair man
She is your bird
Your flower
Set her free
Talk with her
She is a lady
You will over stand

LUCKY

Could this be
True-ness for me
Will she change my life
Take away
Misery
Make me feel special
And keep me happy
Could this be
A true lady
With smarts and wisdom
And also beauty
Kindness understanding
And ability
A lady of the light
And one who can see
I think she is right
And…
A charm for me
Lucky!

LOVE LUCK

Once your heart
Walk through that door
Lock it is
For ever more
In a place
Where
Dear
Comes and no go
To a person
Where
Love
Is tell and show
Creating situations
Of oneness pure
Like never before
A contagious celebration
Of the one you adore
Once
Heart walks
Through that door
Love lock

LONELY

Unused time
And uncovered space
Unfelt love
Grace
And so much dreams waste
It is like
All day long
Being stuck
Strung out on first base
Alone
Your house is not
Your home
Your mind
Is in a different place
Your thoughts just Rome
Your happiness goes
Far as your face
TV won't do
Phone won't do
You needs someone
To feel you through
Lonely is your
Private friend
Happiness seems
To just ignore you
Late at night
When you're alone
Hoping for a knock
Just a ring on the phone
From side to side

To room from room
You roam
By yourself
Doing nothing
Gloom
You're the only one home
Alone
Talking to yourself
Laughing at yourself
Dancing with the broom
Those are
The only good times
You have
When you have no one
You're all alone

LET IT GROW

Like the branches
Of a tree
Let it grow
Like the rays of the sun
It will glow
Like the waters
Of the great seas
You will flow
Like a little girls
First crush
You'll shine
Like never before
Your house will be full
With the colors
Of the rainbow
Just let it grow
Baby let it grow
Let it grow and blossom
Your dreams will come true
And you will
Already know
Your loneliness
Will go away
In your face it will show
I am yours
Yours always
And I'll never
Let you go
Let it grow

KISS AND TENDERNESS

A million roses
For a kiss
A crystal pearl
To make your wish
A heart of gold
For your life of bliss
I'll conquer the world
To defend your weakness
A diamond mine
For your tenderness
A new clothes line
For my mistress
A voyage up in time
For your care-ness
Sweetness
A love divine
For you miss
Tenderness
A kiss
Wish

IN THE SHADOW

My love for you
Will last
Onto the end
My care for you
Is more than that of a friend
The time spent with you
I whole heartedly attend
The beauty i see in you
Is that of a perfect ten
The wonderful things
You do
Have reached
The tip of my pen
Straight is your love
I have not yet seen it bend
From the heavens
Up above
Is where
You have been descend
My love for you
Will last
Longer than the
End

IF YOU DON'T

No smiles
To let it show
No kisses
To let me know
No winks
To make it glow
No hugs
Before I go
No feel
To let it flow
No brushes
When I walk
Through that door
No love
This is not pure
Don't say it
If it is not
So
I can't play it
If love life don't grow
I won't catch it
If you don't throw
My love was high up
Dear
You brought it low
If you can't
Love free me
Baby
Like I be
Let me go
If you don't see

Then I won't show
Baby free me
Let me go

FULL OF FUN

My heart
Is filled with love
True love
The kind
That will always come through
True love
No lies no cheats
No booty in the streets
True love
Always one
Together
The joy, the pain
The rough stormy weather
True love
Happiness as quest
Oneness in eternal rest
True love
Growing into one
Love bright and love bold
Glowing like the sun
Precious diamond as precious gold
Pearls
All everlasting
Loving filled with fun true love
The only one
You

FULL OF FUN

All day long I think of you
You keep me sound
Kools my blue
When you are around
The feel is true
Never let me down
Always come through
Never let me frown
Always know what to do
You bring out my clown
Your happiness
Makes me new
My feet above ground
When I am with you
Booh,
All day long
I'm thinking
Wondering hoping
Waiting for you
It's true

DIVISION

Breaking up
Is hard to do
Waking up
And find it is true
Making up stuff
Without a clue
Taking up enough
For only you
Caking up
When the time comes
To talk thing through
Baking up
The when what the who
Forsake is up
Where through
What am I to do
The fake is up
Love coded blue
The lake is up
The crying is not true
The break is us
One is now two
Breaking up
Is hard to do
Waking up
And say
It is not true
Making up

COLD SHOULDERS

No more soft touching
Seems
Just to smile at me
Is asking
Her too much
No more phone calls
Nothing to say
Seems
We have said it all
No more Friday nights
Our special times
Have taken
A lonely flight
No more long rides
Looking for the treasures
That true love
Hides
No more late night dinners
No more talking
About our lives
Seems it is time
For some one
To start walking
No more sweet words
To each other
Now we hardly look
At one another
No more love
It keeps on getting colder
And I'm sick and tired
Of getting

Your cold shoulder
No more
It seems

CHERRY OF MY EYE

My eyes are for you, Cherrie
Oh how you make me smile
Your incense is true, Cherrie
I smell it all over you
It's been that way for a while
The thought, sight of you
Have controlled brighten my blue
I think it is something
About your style
Dreaded and kind
Full figured and fine
And sweet Cherrie
Intoxicatingly polite
Your effect
It that of fine wine
I'm not drunk Sweet thing
But you staggers my mind
Cherrie, you're sweet
Mind eyes are blind

BLACK ROSE

My beautiful
Black rose
I think
She is the queen of the east
But I am
The only one knows
Like a sleeping beauty
Her royalty
Have been frozen
But still
She shines and glows
Mother of her nature
Everything she touches
It grows
She is the queen
Of this whole wild earth
My beautiful
Beautiful black rose
Is the only one lady
That glows
Upon this world
Of whom my God
Has chosen
For me
A rear black rose

AMERICAN LOVE

Afrikan love
Power love
The most precious love
Ever fall
From above
Rise up now
And show your love
We know love
Faith grows love
From the ground
Straight up above
You've love long
Love grown you strong
It is love
That keeps you around
When their love
Was down
It was you
They found
Make dem sound
Knowing
Your love was around
Now
Trying to bring you down
Your love down
But you are too strong
Love long
Love your ground
Love your song
Love everything
About your towns

Afrika love
Love profound
Afrika love
The most precious love around
Ever fall from above
Afrika love
Sound

A ROSE POSE

My beautiful Black rose
She is a flower in my eyes
In a picture perfect pose
Queen of the flower Rose
I'm the only one who knows
Hidden in the ghetto gardens
Like a sleeping beauty
She dreams of her knight
In time her kingdom has been frozen
She works so hard to find
And still she glows
Mother of her nature
Everything she touches
It grows
She is the queen
Of the garden earth
My beautiful
Perfect black rose
Of whom
I happen to love
Of whom
My heart chose
Black rose

YOUR LOVE HURTS LIKE MINE

Sometimes
You can love
Love too much
You can't get enough
Love
There is too little love
In the world
I say
Once you feel love
It feels too good
It always runs out
Fade away
Leaving jones'
Of love
It comes
In such small supply
Memories of love
The high of love
Always out lasts
The love
Everyone loves
To see loving
So nice and caring
Everyone wants
To be there
Sharing
Happy loving in harmony
When hate is resolved
Love takes victory
That will be a sight
Of love

All will love to see
Your love
And my love
Try my love
Let me try your love
Let's see
If it's all the same
One love
Or just
A trick of the brain
Love

YELLOW DRESS

Yellow is the color of honey
Along with a little black
It is the color of the bees
And sometimes it is the sting
Of knowing someone you love
Can make you feel so good
So damn happy
Free
The color of light as it shows
Rays from the sun making beautiful things grow
Also yellow is the color that you're wonderful
Personality lets go when you smile
And when you laugh, you shine and you glow
Just like the sun
Helping make
Beautiful things grow
It is the
Color yellow
That will last forever
And ever
Never getting old
On top in the rainbow
And in the shine
Of gold
In this color
Yellow I wish
Our relationship
Will grow
And one day
In a yellow dress
Lined with red and green

You will walk
Up slow
With your yellow glow
Be forever
Be my Afrikan queen
Up in wedding row
Bee my honey
Yellow

VALUABLE THING

Once back in time
I had this valuable thing
It made my eyes
Shine
Stare all day
My mind beat ok
It made my life work
Into play
It was so beautiful
But
I lost it all one day
It seems to have just slipped away
Gone, gone, gone
To stay
Come back, come back come back
I pray
But it didn't come back
No way
And then one day
I went out to search
For that valuable
Thing
That made my eyes
Stare all day
My mind thinks
In only one way
And my heart beat
Ok
That made my work
In to play
Started looking

Up and down
Back there over here all around the way
Finally found it
In the Congo
On a good Friday
It made my eyes glow
Stare
Night and day
It made my mind
Think
In only one way
My heart began to sing
My work turn into play
My valuable thing is back
Forever, forever
To stay

TOO TRUE LOVE

True love
Is you love
That is what
You do love
Give it to me true love
No sad
No blue love
Because
I've got you love
Fresh
And brand new love
Nothing we can't do love
Now you are my
Bo love
Gotta do what
We got to do love
No matter what
Or who love
We've got to push
On through love
True love

THE ONE

This bliss
That I feel
So right and so real
Your kindness reveals
An uncompromising
Special deal
And unforgettable sex appeal
I love you
For in love, I will yield
And in writing
I will seal
And in thanksgiving
Tosses
To be a blessed relationship
With the offering of a diamond I kneel
That seals this bliss I feel

ROOF DOWN

An evening ride
On the ocean
With my potential bride
Through the wind
We glide
With a love built pride
Arrogant
Nothing to hide
High
As the tide
With the moon
As our guide
Filling us up
With pure pride
Following the tide
On a most romantic ride
On the ocean side
No emotion hide
Devotion
To my potential bride
Like angels
We glide
Side by side
On a love road ride
On high tide
On high pride
Ocean side
We glide
Moon light guide
Me and my bride
On an evening ride

THE HUNT IS OVER

I have found my baby
No doubt, no fear. no maybe
I was wild already
But she just drives me crazy
She makes me feel just like a star
And every time I make her smile
She lights up like a daisy
She's so pretty and so smart
And her bones are not lazy
But a perfect lady
In my eyes
She just plain out all amaze me
When she's down
You will never know
Never puts on frowns
It never show
When she's happy
She just glow
When I'm with her
I feel pure
Yes my dear
The hunt is over
I have found my heart
In your glow
Over

ROW'S GARDEN

A kiss
A rose
A naked pose
All in loving row's
Open nose
Open doors
Heart full
Cases close
Where all is at will
Emotions flow
The real x pill-ow
Highs equals lows
The garden thrill
Where love buds grow
Learning tender skills
Dreadlocks and 'fros
Feel the chill
Awakening slumbering love
From four hundred years
Snooze
A kiss
A rose
A naked pose
All in loving row's

ONE DIVIDED IN TO TWO

My heart is too good baby
To be wasted
All on you
I have done
All I could
Do
No reasoning
Left to you
My mind have thought
This whole thing through
You have been caught
Your words
Are not true
Your schemes
And your plots
Have made my life
Blue
Real or not
Your games
Are nothing new
You keep me on the spot
You know
I love you
Now the love have
Gone rot
And our hearts have divided
It self
Back in to two
My heart is too good baby

To be wasted all
On you
I've done all
I could
Do

RAIN BOW LADY

Rainbow lady
Your colors
Are so bright
Rainbow lady
With the sweet name knight
You're so kind
Gentle and polite
Rainbow lady
You're so absolutely delight
Lady
Colorful and bright
Every line in order
You hold on to love
So tight
Rainbow lady
You are
A wonder in the sky
Your words your eyes
Your lips no lies
Rainbow lady
Your rays
Cast away my shy
The living sorrows have died
You are the reason why
Rainbow lady
I love to see your glow
You are a sensation
All know
The colors of the sea port
The 39th street rainbow Lady

PURE

Will she be pure
Will she shine
And glow
In the high times
And the low
When there be problems
Will she
Let me know
When the going gets tough
Will she
Still go
When my money is gone
Will she
Share her flow
When I'm all broken down
Will she
Open my doors
When my back aches
Will she
Rub me down
From head to toe
When I want to grind
Get mind
Will she tell me no
When things get bad
Will her love still show
When I tell her no
Will she still remain pure
Will I?

ONE LOVE

Without you in my life, there will be no victory
Without you as my wife, there will be only misery
Pain and sorrow
ill take over me
I will never let that happen
To me
I will take care
Of my responsibility
You have taken my heart
Now I am your responsibility
It has been that way from the start
And have become plain and very visibly
Tearing me apart
That's not hard to see
I have got to be with you
It is written
In our history
The first to find
True love to be free
It will last
Through eternity
Baby
I was made for you
You for me
And Jah wants
The whole world to see
The love we share
Is his love free
And it should be celebrated
In holy matrimony one

NIGHT QUEEN

Night queen brightens up my night
Sweet dreams takes me in to flight
So clean
Erotica is her sight
My queen
She gives me samson might
Sweet dream
Covered in her white
So clean
Put me in her plight
Superbeing
All for my delight
Night queen
Flies me like a kite
Sweet dreams
Snoring
She's all right
So clean
The finest the height
She's mean
Royal and still built tight
She's my queen
On the throne so bright
Sweet dreams
Rainbow by day
Starlit by night
So clean
My queen
Superbeing
Sweet dreams night queen

LOVE LIGHT

How will I know
When I find her
What will love show
Me
To identify her
Will it be beauty
Will it be intelligence
Will it be personality
Or just
Her sweet fragrance
Her style
Or her important
Money or property
What will capture me
What manner of woman
Will fulfill my destiny
How will I know
My queen to be
What signs
Will show
Will she attract me
With a touch
A stare
The song of her voice
Will she be aware
Will I be
Her first choice
Love at first sight
Or first we fight
How will i know
When eye see the light
Will I know
Love sight

LOVE

That cleanness
Of the mind
That sureness
Of the heart
You need to touch
All the time
Don't want to be apart
You're in love
That feeling
Of being bliss
Like a blessing
From above
You float around
All day long
Hanging hovering
Like a dove
You work all day
But it's just like play
This feeling wraps you
Fit you like glove
Holds on to you
You're in love
You see that face
In all the faces
You hear that voice
In all the voices
Thinking of making love
In so many places
You keep
Two
In your thoughts
And two

In your choices
It is totally
Inside of you
Controlling
Your sight your time
Almost everything
You do
No compromising with love
It gets inside of you
It turns you
In to someone else own
It makes you see
Everything new
Your heart stays locked
Mind and view
True
Love was made for two
Adam and eve
Was blessed to receive
The first chance at true love
But Adam was deceived
Since then the world has grieved
And true love has been taken
Back up above

JUST LIKE I

To the queens
Of this earth
I will search for you
My dear
I swear I care
And i am aware
That you are near
Just a peek a stare
A glance of your hair
I know that you're here
I just don't know where
Reveal your self
To me my dear
My heart is the world
And in it
You're spear
Until you
Become my girl
Nothing in it
Will be seen clear
Just one look in your face
And out comes
The spear
Our kingdom will appear
Eternal love
We will both share
To my queen
My dear I swear
Just like you
I care

Just a peek a stare
I'm here
King

I DO

Yes I do
I do love you
I think your words
And heart is true
I hope
That I can
Continue seeing you
Doing things
With you
What you love
To do
Meet all of your friends
Make them
My new
Take away your sorrows
Bad feeling and blues
Be there for you
For your tomorrow
Number one
In your crew
Just say the word baby
The way you say
It's
True
I am a real man
And I feel
You coming through
Yes I do

GOOD POETRY

Already
I can see
You bring out the best in me
It is written
That you are
Good poetry
So much to write about
You arouse my fantasy
Brings out the best in me
Your smiles are ecstasy
I want you next to me
I'll write
You lines of poetry
Shower my mind
With love fancy
Make you mine
Start a dynasty
Put you in a rhyme
Poetry
Girl you're made
For me
Already I can see

FIRST MAN

In this war
You are my first man
Upon this friendship
You are
The whole damn crew
It was just me baby
And now
It is just us two
Up against
The whole damn world
Right now
But pulling through
Love times makes new
The world would lose
Up against
Me and you
In 2008
Love mysteries
Will be solved
Our love will hold
All the mysteries clues
You are
Sunshine in my life
Together our lights
Will continue
Never ending true
My heart knew
Before my
Mind came to
My eyes kept seeing

The good inside of you
Our love is divine
And it has surely grew
True thoughts
Through times
Everlasting is the meaning
Of true

DOUBLE BACK

Eye came back
To see you to
I like
What eye see to
I like your smiles
I like your styles
I wonder
If you can drive me wild
Take this number
And take a while
When you remember
You're finished with carl
Give me a dial
Make me smile
Turn me on
To your new style
Let me dial
Drive you wild
Find out what
Is my grove style
Eye
Came back to
See you to
I like what eye
Saw to
Double back

DAVID STAR

Afrikan bird
Your voice songs sweet
Every time
I see your face
My heart picks up
A beat
And your color
I just adore
Amazing figure your grace
And always
You dress so neat
You are a beauty
Of our race
Dark and lovely
A light in the street
A star
You shine in David's place
So pretty
Soon I hope
We will meet
And share together
Some time and space
To see rather
We cold out
Or warm up and create heat
Afrikan bird
My eyes on you
And I would like to fly
With you
Low and high
Glide with you

Just name your fun
Your wish
As commanded
I will do
Afrikan bird
I fly true

BRILLIANT MIND

I can see you are
An intelligent woman
A brilliant mind
Could you give me
A moment
To see what's
In mind
From the minute
I saw you
You have been
Controlling my mind
I really adore you
I see you are fine
Only me and you
Our kind
Is only two
I heard your heart is true
A brilliant mind
Baby mine is to
I have many more lines
What you gonna do
Are you gonna be mine
One and one is two
I see you are
A nine

All depends on how you do
You will get one more
If you're kind
My attention has grown
On you
Now I see
You are a dime
Baby me and you
Simple
As red wine
To find each other's true
Same heart and same mind
Nothing left to do
Make this love divine
I can see that
You're intelligent to
A brilliant mind

AS YOU ARE

Who loves me
As I am
Who loves me
Caught up in the jam
Who loves me
Son of ham
Who loves me
They say I am damned
Who loves me
I slay the vamp
Who loves me
Like peter pan
Who loves me
As I am
Who loves me
Caught up in this jam
Who loves me
Damn

TEXT OR CALL

Late in the evening
When the day
Begins to fall
I think of another night
Without seeing
You at all
And the sorrow
Begins to call
Saying to me
I have got to be free
I have got to break through
These distance walls
Because day after day
As time slips away
I wonder
I think
I should give it
My all
I know it is so
I don't think
That she know
But I still think so
She is such
A baby doll
So fine and so sweet
So neat and so kind
She wipes away my sorrow
Whenever she text
Or she gives me a call
She is a sweet lady
She makes my love fall

SPECIAL LADY

A special lady
Just like I said
And a beautiful one to
A special lady's only
Can do
The thing you do
Don't think
That this is lust
That I see and feel
In you
Your beauty
And your charms
Are just two things
Of a few
But it is your heart and drive
I have been seeing
You through
Don't change anything
It's working baby
It takes
A very special lady
To do the thing you do

JOY

You are
What happens
When everything
Goes right
Instantly
You attracted
Me
And then
You took
My sight
Soon
I started to see
I had joy in me
And things started
Then
To look very bright
So i thank you joy
For making
Right my day
With your kind smiles
In such
A very friendly way
You are the kind of lady
Unto Jah
I pray
A joy

HIS QUEEN

His love is divine
And his quest is royalty
He search
In hope to find
Someone with faith
And loyalty
That will honor him
All the time
In total respect
And morality
Her heart must be
Both clean and kind
To be
Mother to the family
One love
Unconditionally
And color blind
One love onto infinity
Perfect lady
Let your tree be seen
Shine
And ever lasting
Your colors
Will be green
On a throne for ever
It will reign
Only you can bring
Prosperity
To where there is now
Pain

He could only be king
If first
You be his queen

GONE, GONE

When the thrill is gone
How do you carry one
The day lights
Of love is gone
Now it is darkness
And you're feeling
All alone
Lord
I have been warned
But now my heart
Can feel the scorn
Like a woman's pain
When a child is born
The only thing
That can help me now
A fifth of patron
My attitude
AL Capone
Go to do something crazy
To make this pain
Leave me alone
Thinking about
The days
When our love was
In the zone
Now I'm here in a maze
Baby the thrill is gone
Wondering

Into tomorrow
How can I go on
Hearing voices
On my phone
The nights of love
Have dawn
I can't leave my home
I feel the feel of scorn
Damn
The thrill is gone

EYES AND EARS

At first
Hearts
Can't see heart
So what gets
The everlasting love start
Love at first sight
Seeing
The figure
Figures the shape the art
Voices the songs
Does true love come
Through the ear
Then gets inside the heart
How and where
Ture love is start
Eyes and ears
Art
Creates feelings
Starts

DREAM FANTASY

I don't have
No friends you see
No one have
The respect for me
When I'm down
I'm there with
Nobody
No one there
To feel me
When I'm happy
No one's there
To share my candy
It's not fair
That I am so sad
Lonely
It's like no one is there
To get
To know me
I have no sugar baby
I'm just waiting
Here
On my love
My dream fantasy

DEEP AND WILD

My love flows deep
As the wells
Far back as the Nile
Of the voices
In the shells
Within the beast of the wild
A bond of unbreakable spells
Two mended into
One style
Memory of songs
In the scents the smells
Can't wait to gaze
A loving smile
Love always shows
Faith always tell
Going the extra miles
Infinity
Ringing the binding bells
Adding to the scene
Creating us into a child
All together
Under love clouds
We dwells
Love dreams begin
With you and I baby
I am into you
Whole heartedly
Save me
It flows deep

CHOSEN

Love of my friends
In life
And now
Time has made you
My love
She is my lady
And she loves it my way
I love it hers
She is in my heart
To stay
She is my chosen queen
And there's no price
I won't pay
To be with her
Forever
Forever and even every day
I will love and honor her
Practice that I pray
I'll lead her
And follow her
And Jah will guide our way
Sunrise with her
Sunset with her
Slow walks across the bay
Crabbing in the creek
With her
Late nights in the streets
Down in the lows
With her
High as the milky way
You see

Our love goes deep
And it's getting
Higher every day
Our love is whole for keeps
Long after old and grey
Chosen

APART-MENT

We have been
Fighting from the start
Now the fight
Have reach my heart
And I think
We should part
At night you and I
We're just too smart
Instead of love
It is martial art
Instead of peace
We come apart
At the lease
A fire start
Expired lease
No feast
A broken heart
It just increase
And grows apart
Our love have cease
Among the depart

STAR

I saw that star
It seem so near
But yet so far
And it winked at me
I took it as a message
From Jah
Telling me that I have found
A star
Treat it right
And you will go far
So I winked back
And got on my knees
And gave thanks
And praises to Jah
For sending me
Such a very bright star
I will shine her everywhere
No place will be too far
She will be in my heart
Always
Next to Jah
In my mind all day
And at night
My star
The space in between us
Somehow seems
To far
But it won't be too long
I wish upon Jah
I saw the star

TAKE TIME AND DO IT

There's nothing
Here to see baby girl
I love blind
You see
What you want of me
Baby girl
It takes time
Reality or fantasy
What is your line
For money or for me
Baby girl
What is your sign
Love or ecstasy
What your taking
For the mind
Baby girl
Work or all party
How you getting up your grind
Kids
One two or three
How much lovers
You left behind
A lady
Is it just me
How much will I find
Religion
Is your faith free
Or you eating
Off the swine
Education elementary

Or you're bright
As you are fine
Patient
Do you have it for me
Or it's all just
About the good times
Your mama
Is she unhappy
When you give a player
Too much of your time
Your daddy
Will he cap me
If you tell him
I hit that fat behind
Other wise
There is nothing here to see
Baby girl
I love blind

OUR PART

Hurricane tornado
Snow storm quake
Lightening thunder
Volcano bake
Hail storm forming
Warming fire lake
Flooding on the rise
How much more
Can we take
Drought taking
Over the land
Are we all being
Forsake
Drugs and deceases
Are the worst of all
Disasters
Man himself makes
Think about it
A great wake
When I do
It makes me shake

LEAVE

A single leaf
From a tree full of leaves
Green
A message i believe
A single leaf
Falling from a green tree
Just one
Fell in front of me
A leaf from the family tree
Fallen
To the ground lonely
But still under the tree
I wonder
If the wind will come for me
And take me
Back to my family kin tree
A single leaf

SAGITTARIUS

Hi
The gardens are turning
The air is cooling
By the north eastern wind
Snakes and insect are
Turning in
Bears to the den
Grass in the fields
Are brittle
And thin
Leaves are falling
Their time have been
The cold is calling
Bring autumn in
Taking away
The hot summer days
Until we meet
Again
At the cancer lines
Again
Good bye cancer

ROSE

Oh how beautiful
A rose
The sign of budding love
I suppose
That only true love
Knows
With the fragrance
Of freshness
And from the thought
Love grows
Oh how beautiful
A rose
As a untimely gift
My love in the presence
It is a rose
Pit of the places
Where only true love
Flows
Deep red like blood
And upon a throne it glows
Oh how beautiful
A rose
A symbol of love and friendship out of many
She has been chose
The flower that sticks
And makes her smile
Glow
Oh how beautiful
How beautiful
My rose

RECYCLE

Spring water springs
Clean clear purified
Up from under the rocks reaching up
To the clear blue skies
Forming clouds
Until thunder knocks
Then
Drip, drip, drip
Drops
Back down
From heavens high
On its way
Back down
Through the rock
Rain water springs
When nature cries
Purifies

RAIN BOW

I see the beauty
That
Rein through the sky
When the sun shines down and the rain passes by
Leaving a bow
Or maybe it's an eye
Red orange green and yellow
The colors that glows
When nature cries
It never stays long
As if through a wink
A wink from mother eye
Appears in the sky
And gone in a blink
One half above ground
And the other half
Below
When I see the rain bow
It always makes me think
Of the half
Below
It seems to be
A missing link
Some says
It points out gold
Some says
Fresh water to drink
Maybe one day
We will all know
What is the secret
Beyond the rain bow

The colors in the sky
In perfect circles
All in a row
That stops the time
Takes the show
Look up there behold
A rain bow
It is always the same
Where ever you go
People stop and stare
Whenever there's
A rainbow
Or maybe it is an eye
Staring back

QUEEN DE-NILE

Black mild
Full of style
Drives me wild
No denial
A hypnotically
Unchallenging smile
From the Niles
Black mild
Judgment a ten
Hung the jury up
On trial
Top of the pile
She will reconcile
Read the ancient
Files
Beautiful
Black and mild
A lady of the Nile

THE PASS PRESENT FUTURE

21 oaks
On your birthday
21 oaks
For the strength
You have display
21 oaks
For many green years
As long as you
Want to stay
21 oaks
You're baby tears
And memory
How we laugh
And play
21 oaks
For your birthday
Nothing
Could ever
Blow them away

OUR MOTHER

Mother earth
We have hurt you so
Covering up
And polluting
Where your beautiful gardens
Once grow
Cutting you down
And digging you out
Faith in Jah
Is dangerously low
Creating bombs
Of fire and germs
That will genocide your whole family
No matter where
They live or go
How long
Will you let this go on
In your house
Mom
Motherly love
Before you close
Your Heavenly doors

WHY NATURE?

Today is a good day to fly
Through the open sky
Or swim the open sea
Because I'm feeling
So fresh
And free
Or maybe I will climb
A mountain
A tree
And feel
That feeling high
Take a walk
Through
A beautiful rain forest
By the wells
Where the fresh waters
Springs by
On the lake
In a canoe
With my baby
Rowing through nature
Why?

WATER SHIP

Clouds rolling by
Slowly through the air
An abstract in the sky
On its way
To create an atmosphere
Will it fade away
And die
Or go let rain fall
Out somewhere
Joining figures
Way up high
Or vanish disappear
Calmly floating by
Like a ship
As it drift
To the pier
Does anyone knows why
In the clouds
Lightning and thunder
Flares
Because when clouds fly
It's direction
Is never clear
They just
Roll slowly by
Transforming
Abstract
In the air

TOMORROW

The birds
And the bees
The sky the mountains
Flowers and the trees
All the fish in the seas
The snow and the rain
The cool breeze
The fountain drains
The river freeze
Hills and valleys
Grass so green
Dessert wide
And river long
Wind whispering
A sorrowful song
Cloud adrift
Beneath the stars
Eagle a seek
It's prey from afar
Mankind peaks
What comes tomorrow
Animal a prey
Being preyed upon
Today he lose
Yesterday he won

TOMMY ROSE BUD

Beautiful black rose
You're so fine
All can see
You're bright
You shine
You glow
So kind to me
I wonder
If you know
Your fragrance
A mystery
In gardens where you grow
Your presence
A fantasy
Beautiful black rose
I think that you
Have been cut out
For me
Rose

THUNDER BIRD

Summer bird
Singing from a tree
Sounding so sweet
And free
If her songs were words
I wonder
What it would be
The songs
I have heard
Coming from that
Sweet bird
Sounded like
A prayer for me
I didn't say a word
I just listen
And the voices
Was joined by three
First second and a third
Singing mysteriously
Sweet harmonies
Summer birds
Singing a melody
Singing songs
That is never heard
Meant for me
Until
You listen to it
Faithfully
Gracefully
Thunder birds

THE ONLY GOOD

It's Friday
And I can see the sun rising
It's Friday
And I feel the week ending
It's Friday
And I see my day of resting
It's Friday
And I see my money spending
It's Friday
And I see my day of praying
It's Friday
And I feel my day of blessing
It's Friday
And I see the children playing
It's Friday
It's time for us to go fishing
It's Friday
Break out the grill and lets go cooking
Good old Friday
And I feel the week is ending

THE FALL

August have gone
And September is here
The time of fall
Is drawing near
The north winds are calling
The warm weather birds
And flowers
Will soon disappear
And fade gray
Cold
Will begin
It's slow roll
Straight through
The first of the new year
But for now
September is here
And the skies
Are still blue and clear
Bright everywhere
But a cold breeze
Sends chill through the air
Baseball play offs
Football in gear
Nascar
Halloweens around the corner
Thanksgiving
Prepare
Christmas time
A time of loving
Sharing
The cool is coming
Autumn flair

It is the fall
Of the 2008 year
August is gone
And September is here

THE GARDENS COLOR

Dark and lovely
Mysterious but kind
From the start of my day
Onto the night
Finish line
Your name
Your beauty
Your color
Your fragrance
Are the first
And the last thoughts
That goes through my mind
One color black
From head to toe
Chocolatey smooth
With curves and angles
That does things
On its own
That you couldn't possibly know
You're like
Someone from the future
That is here
And i know
Maybe you are
A princess

Or even maybe an Afrikans queen
No matter what
Or who
You're the most beautiful black
I have ever seen
Uncut pure and original
Special just like
Eve
Rear a black rose
Yes
Black and beautiful
Don't even let
Your self be deceived
Stay proud Afrikan lady
For the colors
Are the first
And it was a seed in your gardens
Jah gave us birth

THE HIGHER DECK

Rainbow river
More than 2,000 miles
From shore to shore
With colors
In your smile
Your blue current forever flows
From the mountain
Straight through the nile
New waves
To let all know
We are coming home
In style
Upon the bridged rainbow
In a whirl wind
Blowing wild
Afrikan wild
No one will be chained below
Shackle
Stack pack in piles
River rainbow
The moon will be
Brought low
We are crossing you this time
In style
Still black and still mild

TIME CARRIES

Time carries on
Till dawn
Unstopping just changing
Until the last minute is gone
Adjusting and arranging
Until time cup
Is over flowing
Every day revealing
It's oneness
By worn
Today given beauty
Tomorrow it is scorn
Taken from one
And in another it is born
Two time
All creation is as simple
As an ear of corn
Come and gone
A scale to the end
By all
Time is sworn
Nothing like time
It ticks
It warns
Time carries on

TO THE LETTER

Mocking bird
Can you come out
To play
Your sweet songs
In your special way
Can you say what I say
Mocking bird
Don't fly way
I love to see
Your beautiful
Black and gray
I love to hear
The songs you sing
In my yard each day
Mocking bird
Your songs are dear
Mark every word I say

MY TOMORROW

The time have pass
Tomorrow
Is drawing near
Today was o.k.
But tomorrow
Is almost here
Yesterday
Seems so far away
But today
Is the day
Before tomorrow
Already I feel
The ending
To my sorrow
I can't wait to see
My baby smile tomorrow
Day have come
And days will go
But I just can't wait
For my sweet
Tomorrow
The day I have
Been longing for so
Watching the minutes of the hours
Moving along so slow
But the time is almost here
My day is tomorrow
Tomorrow, tomorrow
My day is tomorrow

TWO FACED LOVE

The sun flower
Raises its head
To the sun
Watches it
Spread
Rise and fall
With a smile
On its face
All day long
But at night
Their heads hang down
In the morning
It lifts
Again
It turns around
And waits for the sun
To take away
It's frown
Then follow it again
From ground to ground
Head hung down
Shedding
The seeds of tears
All done wrong
By the darkness
Affairs

WELL

Water fresh
Water clean
Water flowing
Clear as air
From the great rain
Down
The mountains stream
Into the earth vain
Purified and restrain
Up through the well
Breaking thirst
And the drought
Spells
No one remembers
When that rain fell
Above or below
Holy water wells

ONE TEAR

One tear
Is all I have
For the eyes shut
Leaders
And the millionaires
One tear
Is all I can spare
For the murderess
Drug dealer
In their
Die society atmosphere
One tear
Without sincere
For the racist and prejudice
And haters any
And everywhere
One tear
With no love or care
For the starters of war
The polluters of air
The filthy rich
Whom wants more
And the slave wage payers
They are not fair
One tear
Crystal clear
For the cheaters
Of another
And for him
He whom just stare
The beaters of babies

And the judgment declare
One tear
A single flair
To the listener
Whom there not hear
The see'er
That closes their ear
For the poor baby
The sufferer
Many tears
My heart eye dear
Eyes cry all year
One tear

NATURE

Simple beauty
Un-ask for love
A Godful duty
Below and above
Gardens so fruity
Skies full with dove
Good weather
Ruff
Clear
Moody
The earth replenish itself
Call of the wild booty
Boys and girls
Gifts of love
Nature is a Godful duty
The worms below
The eagle high above
The garden in between
Love everlasting beauty
The raging war
The angel soft cries
Of a baby dove
Low and high tide
Unstable and moody
Nature is a duty
It's call love
Simple beauty
Un-ask for love
Nature

MY SOUTH

Rivers flowing
Fresh and clean
Wind blowing
Air
Clear and clean
Grass growing soft and green
Pollen pouring
Down like rain
Gardens sowing
Fresh veggie and grain flower showing
The fruit tree leans
Farmers hoeing
Weed
From the bean
Children throwing rocks in the stream
Rooster crowing
Awake in your dream
Pond echoing
The sounds
Of the whooping crane
Home team scorning
In a down south
Ball game
There is no snowing
A little hail
Lot of rain
Ask any one knowing
It is a down south scene
We keep it glowing
In our voices
Scream

It's in our vein
My south clean
Carolina green
My south

MOSS AND WISDOM

Acorns
Are raining down
Under the great oak tree
Wisdom
On its way to the ground
To start
A great journey
It won't be long
Before the seed
Becomes a great
Grand tree
Growing strong
For many, many century
Shading
Rooting the grounds
For many, many family
Just an acorn
An oak's baby
Lives so long
The grand pappy
Mammy
Raining down
Under the great
Mossy oak tree

LOVE DAY

Today
Is a good day
To love
Because today is
Love's birthday
The beginning of love
Is on this day
Angels and doves
Deliver love from above
Between two hearts
It loveliness lay
Cradle by love
And fed love
And prayers all day
Manna from above
Protected
From love
Prey
The nourishment of love
Of a tender baby
Born on this day
It is love's birthday
Today
Is a good day to love
All day
Let it grow
Flow
Glow
I pray

SAVANNA

Afrika in Savanna
Where the lioness
Is the bread winner
She hunts
She protects
And leads the pride
Reflex
She collects
The morning manna
Respected
The lioness never fears
Or hides
Queen of the beast
The Afrikan banner
First to tear the feast
Pride
Lurks in the Savanna
When I reach
Her territory
I will make of her
My bride
Queen of my pride

ROSEY DREAMS

Roses as your pillow
Kisses
In your dreams
Sweet words
Love
For your tender
Heart
With the passion
Of a scream
Understanding
For your giving part
The will
To give the same
To make this love
A winning start
Without finish
Or with out
Heart pains
To me baby
You are the gardens
Beauty
In feminine art
You hypnotically
Attract my brain
And simplicity
Attack my heart
In my dream
I am a garden
Baby
And you're love
Brings me rain
Rosey dream

ROOSTER

Rooster crows
At working time
What he knows
To the rest
Is blind
Out of the nest
Get the easiest find
Cock a doo
From the chest
Wake up caller
On the line
Dawn in the east
Same time
Dust in the west
A minute to the hour
Thinking mind
Rooster crow
And tell time
What roosters know
The second is divine
Tic crock tic crock tic crock
Right on time

REFLECTION

When the moon is full
At night
When the skies
Are blue and bright
The tide will flow
Over the normal height
Love arrows
Will be bowed
High into flight
Hidden features
Will be found
Within the light
Some people will get mean and ugly
And others
Will be polite
Some will get joyful
And
Others will be uptight
The creature creeps
The hunter hunts
The lover tests his might
In the full moon
To the night
The sky will be
Beautiful and bright
When the moon is full
At night

RECESS

Summer have arrive
And gardens
Are coming alive
The birds are flying
Everywhere
The bees are building
Brand new hive
The animals are out
A live
For the seasons
To catch some fresh air
Thank Jah
They make it through the winter
Alive
The beaches are all open
Every where
Everyone is taking
A dive
Children all out side
Playing with friend
From nine up to five
Husband are marrying
Wives
The happiest
Are the summer bride
All of nature
Begin to strive
Hot weather features
Comes alive
Vacation for the teachers
Summer
Have arrive

RAINBOW EXPLOSION

Indeed a charm
One with grace
That bloom
That alarms
I need a charm
A lucky charm
To protect me
From hurting harm
Keep me calm
A winning charm
A beautiful leprechaun
With sweetness of gold
That have
No scorn
With brightness behold
A charming and full of charm
A loving alarm
And an explosive self
None the less calm
The bomb
Are you
My beauty charm

RAIN AND SUNSHINE

The rain is falling
The sun is shining
Rainbow
In the sky
Colorful lining
With beauty so binding
Stares you in your eyes
Rain and sunshine comes
Together
Brings out the beauty
In the sky
When the mind eye meets
My sunshine
Colorful we will fly
Over the rainbow
Way up high
To bury our love
With the treasures
In the sky
You and I
Rainbows

THE BIRDS AND THE BEES

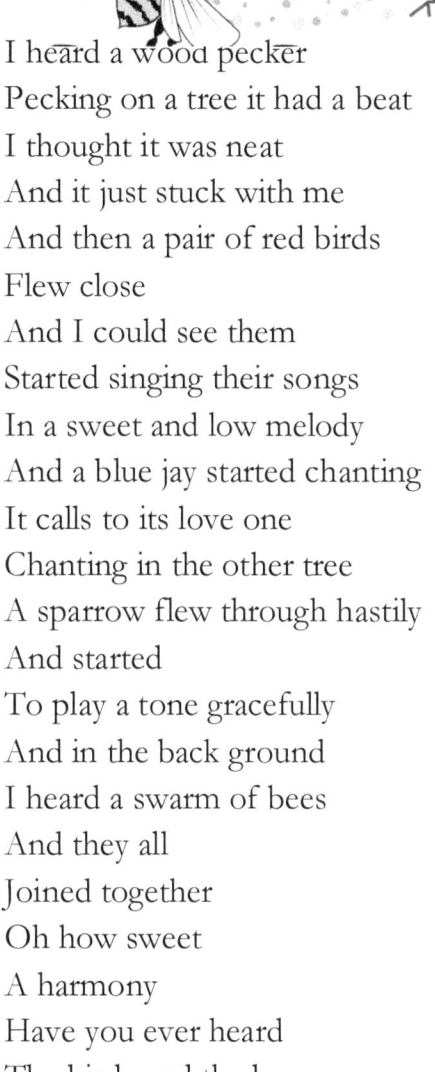

I heard a wood pecker
Pecking on a tree it had a beat
I thought it was neat
And it just stuck with me
And then a pair of red birds
Flew close
And I could see them
Started singing their songs
In a sweet and low melody
And a blue jay started chanting
It calls to its love one
Chanting in the other tree
A sparrow flew through hastily
And started
To play a tone gracefully
And in the back ground
I heard a swarm of bees
And they all
Joined together
Oh how sweet
A harmony
Have you ever heard
The birds and the bees

KNOCKING RAIN

Rain
You are my lady love
I will always love you
Rain
I wait for your knocks
Upon my roof top
So I can open my mind
And let you in
With your ticking songs
It makes me wonder
When I hear it
Again and again
Sometimes
You roll like thunder
Some say rain
Sometimes
That you are mean
But I love you
Always the same
You take away
My pain
Blocks the rays
Of the hot dry sun
Waters down the grains
Every time you cry
Some things are lost
But more are gain
I'm always sad
When you say
Goodbye
That is when

I feel my pain
I love you rain
Can't wait for you to knock again
Knock – knock - knock

I DREAM OF AN AFRIKA

In a dream
Truly to me she came
Afrika was her name
She took me in
A love domain
I never felt the same
My heart was taken
My mind was shaken
She started up a flame
Burning with beauty pleasure
And ecstasy
And desire
I didn't want to tame
Wild love
Felt it in my brain
My heart was overcame
With joy
I never felt the same
Afrika
You are my love
My smiles my fears my shame
All conquered
When your queenship came
My true love
Met my dream

And you love
In the fame
Is for you love
I will beam
Never give up your flame
I'll make my life
A dream
Truly to me she came
Afrika was her name
In my dream

HIDDEN IN THE GARDEN

Hello mother ever
Why did you
See it fit to deceive
Our father Adam
Whom in Jah
Believe
In faith and love
And knowledge to achieve
But now
The whole world
Is lost and shame filled
With grief
And still
We hide our sins
With broken garden leaves
Why?

GROWING LOVE

my heart
is driven
by the unfortunate
pain
it feels
the living
pumps blood
through my veins
honest and forgiving
it comes down sometime
like rain
all over the world
like green
I love all
all is my friend
when my heart
meets yours
I will surely
increase
my love
once again

GOOD EVENING

Evening breeze
Flowing
Slowly through
The sun is going down
And the cool of the night
Is dew
Summer days
Are hot and long
But evening time
Comes
It all calms down
As the dark shades
Are drew
The in between lines
Of a day getting old
And a night born
Fresh and new
When the eternal
Unwind
And the nocturnal eyes
Begins to shine
The two
Is in passage
Time
Awake is all creatures
And kind
When the evening breeze
Comes slowly through
The sun is gone
Down
And the cool of the night
Is dew

SPRING HAND

The birds are singing
The skies are clear
School bells
Are not ringing
Spring break is here
Love ones are clinging
Some thing
Is in the air
Flowers
Will be bringing
This season cannot
Be compared
Pollen will be hanging
From branches
Everywhere
Wild grass will be springing
And the buds starts to appear it is spring time
Once again
A time when nature
Does her planning
For the coming year

FALLING STARS

The night
Is on the rise
As the day light
Slowly dies
Without a fight
His brightness
Slowly dries
And then darkness
Rise
With tall shadows
And hidden surprise
Hollow echo
Of the sleepless cries
Creepers on the move
From down low
Seeking highs
Peekers in their grove
The stars are bright
Up in the sky
The bars are open
Collecting lies
The parks
Getting full
With strange looking guys
And the wolf
Wears wool
In the hunt
For the pleasure
Of their eyes
When night rise
Day light
Dies

ENDANGERED

Forest gardens
The rain brings it
Fresh water
The wind brings fresh air
The sun shines new rays
Lightning flashes thunder fears
The tide rises but never stays
The young having fun
Playing and the old thinks
While the animals
Grow endanger
The great forest weakens
Shrinks
No more fresh air
The sun rays
Are getting dangerous
The tides are climbing higher
Dropping lower
Lightning and thunder
Tornado
Is drawing from afar
Drawing near
Young men
Pay attention
Old men
Stay in tune
The elements
Is telling the story
The time for
Jah come soon

DO IT FOR LOVE

My love is not for one people only
My love is not for one race only
My love is stated
All is equal
I love people
Love
All human faces
My love is universal
Covers all spaces
Domestic and commercial
Heroes
On the arm force bases
Love is not reversal
Same alike
Religion
Same alike
In all places
Love practice
Love rehearsal
All neighbors
Must be embraced
Spirits invisible
Love is the only sin
One never pray to have erase
My love is universal
With love
I rest my case
For all the people
Of the human race

DEW DROPS

Does the gardens
Cry at night
When the sin
Takes away
It's light
She hold
Her head down
A motion uptight
With hidden frowns
For light she longs
All through the night
Crying until dawn
In the dark
Without her sight
All alone
No sun no might
For the gardens throne
Does she cry out at night
And smiles
All day long
Sweet flower what's
Wrong

DEFINITION

Zion is our destination
Everlasting is our celebration
Love is our motivation
Peace is our desperation
Faith is our inspiration
Care is our education
Fear of the Lord is our inner-sensation
Definition

CONCERT

Evening rain
Comes falling down
Washes away
The dry hot day
Cools the heated ground
Water
For the sun burnt grass
But the evening rain
Don't stay long
Flooding every hole
Within it pass
The lightning flash
The thunder sounds
Never last
But comes through fast
With turbulence
So massive
Profound
Weatherman forecast
Evening rain
But no one really knows
What goes down
Behind evening rain
Forces of nature
Rocks the ground
With the band of thunder
Lightning volt
Shock songs
At the volume
Of wonder
The evening rain
Show
Is throwing down

OF FEATHERS

Beautiful birds
Came by my yard today
Wood peckers sparrows
Cardinals blue jays
All came by
To see that
I was ok
Singing their songs
Scratching away
From the tree limb
To the ground
The song they play
Flying around and around
Preparing their nests
To lay
Singing family songs
Sang
In a special way
A pair of each
Came by my yard
Today
Red yellow black bird brown
Blue jay
Like a rainbow
They all flew away
Beautiful birds
Came by today

IN BETWEEN US

Today
Was a dreary one
The clouds came
And blocked the sun
Today
Was a dreary one
A little wind
A little rain
But a lonesome scene
The sun didn't come
It was a dreary one
This day was
A day
Unhappiness
Will be done
No light to spark
The play
The clouds
Have blocked the sun
It didn't come
Today was dreary
One
The colors had a run
The flowers
They had none
The butterflies
Did not come
A dreary one
A misty one
Today
The sorrow won

COLOR OF LOVE

Let your little boys and girls
Go and play
Make sure you teach them
The playful way
Keep them in your sight
The whole day
Always be there
If just to say
I love you
In that special way
With hugs and smiles
Baby it's ok
Our babies are not bad
That is just the way
Called children play
Don't let them be sad
By words you might say
About another child parent
Or the way they pray
The kids are all blind lovers
So let the children play
And stay
Out of their way

SUNDAY EVENING

It is Friday morning
The air is fresh
The skies are clear
The sun
Is on the rise
The weekend
Is finally here
The last day
Of hard work
Time to collect our fares
Rest on Saturday
Enjoy the atmosphere
When Sunday morning comes
Our best work starts
On our knees
Praying to Jah
A pray
For another week
Of good health
And true love
Wisdom for all
To share
Until Friday morning
Passes over again
I hope our air
Stays fresh
And the skies
Stays clear
And clean

STORY TELLER

Old man oak
Your limbs are so strong
You have been sitting there
For so very long
Over four hundred years
Now
Tell us
What went wrong
Your roots goes very deep
Your massive and profound
So tell us
From your early days
When you was first
Put to the ground
How you became so
Full of wisdom
And still manage
To stand around
How can you stay
So green
All the time
When all the rest of the
Leaves and falling down
Old man oak
What is your eternal secrets
What keeps you so damn sound

SPRING AIR

Feel it in the air
The time of spring
Is near
Days are getting warmer
Flowers blooming
Every where
The kids are getting ready
For spring break
Is almost here
The birds are singing
In pairs
Pollen dust floating
Everywhere
The signs if spring
Is clear
Nature turns green
Flowers light up the scenes
Spring time
Is in the air
Bees and butterfly
Come out from their hiding
The cold is gone
There's nothing to fear
Spring is the only season
That shows how much
Nature really cares
She always comes back
Faithfully
Same time each year
And every year
To put back

The green lights
Into the gardens
After summer fall and winter
Have taken away
The flare
And made to fall down
Brown and bare
Spring is in the air

SOUL MEMORY

It is like
A bicycle ride
Or that swim
In the open sea
Life is just a glide
Like elementary
Drifting with the tide
When every one's
Free
Of all
Racial guide
From past history
The truth
Should not hide
It is in our country tree
The nation shame and pride
Should be remembered
Permanently
Like our first bicycle ride
The first swim
In the sea
Like mom me
A soul memory

SEVEN SENSE

I can think of the Creator and meditate among His stars
See the day light and the darkness of the night
Smell the roses
The fruits of the gardens as they grow
Taste the manna, veggies underground, potatoes
The tree grows fruit
Bananas
Hear the songs
The cheerful noise coming from the nouns
Feel the world
The soft cool cloud
The hardened pearl and love
The most beautiful girl
With all the senses given to me from knowledge
Way up above
I think
I see
I smell
I hear
I feel
I taste
I love
All in seven senses

MS. TOMORROW

Words of sorrow
The feeling of
Hollow
Is the thoughts
That yields
When I think of tomorrow
Being without you
No love to follow
My pathway
Narrow
Through my heart
Sorrow
I can't think
Hollow
All my happiness
Borrowed
Loneliness
Follow
Oh my bliss
Narrow
I already miss
Tomorrow
Lord I miss tomorrow

GARDENS ARE BEAUTIFUL

Flowers in the garden
Beauty and fragrance
Growing, growing out
From the soul
With a thorn
So hardened
But the face
Of nature baby doll
Up to the sun
All day staring
Nodding from sunrise
Onto the fall
Your colors so many
So bold
So bright
So good for
Begging your pardon
A natural grown light
Attracts us all
The essence of pure sight
Seen in the garden
In the face
Of a flower
Soft
Harden
Beautiful power

CARE

My cup runneth over
With drops of tears
When eye see
The unnourished Afrikans
Living out their life
In just a few years
No food no doctor
And no clean water
While the whole world looks on
In simplistic stares
But just waiting for time
To make it disappear
My cup runneth over
With my relative blood
Suffering over there
Dripping
Back into the dirt
Living their whole life
Knowing only fear
Who care
Maybe it is the raft
Of our god worth
But why do we have
So damn much over here
Our cup runneth over
In to the land
Of the most millionaire
That is why
I always keep the rich
In my sympathy
And in my prayer

For my blood is spilled
Afrika
Over there
My cup runneth over
With every drop of tear

BLEEDING HEART

The weight
Of my heart
Causes it to overflow
And then it starts to bleed
For all the ugly in this world
And in the stories
The books I have red
My heart bleeds
For little boys and girls
That will be born
Innocently
Into this world
Of the poor poorer
And the greedy greed
How they come so
Innocently
Until their life
Is half spent
To find one self
Following the wrong lead
My heart bleeds
It overflows
On love it feeds
My heart bleeds

BACK DOWN

Cut back
On them chicken boy
Cut back
On them hog girl
'Dem damn cows
Are so damn mad
We kill them
Before we kill a dog
They give us milk
Eat weed
And fertile out grass
Cut back
On the frogs
Cut back
On the animal eating
And pay attention
To our natural gardens
Turning into
Old dried logs
Suffering from the acid rain
And covered up
By the smoggy smog
Cut back
On the meat
Don't cut down our trees
Let the animal go
Let the gardens grow
Before
None be no more
Back down neighbors
Let them go
Let Earth grow

CLOUD'S SHIPS

Floating around
Like ship's
In the sky
Changing shapes
As you slowly drifts by
Sometimes
A dragon
Sometimes
A butterfly
I have seen things
In you
I could not
Believe my eyes
Your secrets are heavenly
And it rains
When you cry
The guiding angels
To earth
You store
Our water supplies
And upon your surface
Is where everyone
Wants to be
Upon that day
We're numbered to die
Sailing around
Like ships
In the sky

BLOOMING BRIDE

To the flower
Which is my bride
Of whom
I have decide
To pay attention
And to abide
To treat with passion
Long and wide
Dress in fashion
Beach walks
On high tide
From our love mansion
With loving neighbors
On both sides
In your garden
Babies
We will plant seeds
Our pride
You are my queen
Flower
My forever blooming bride

OMEGA

Land of the tree
Where budding love
Should be
Prosperity
Land of the free
The garden's tree
Fruit of eternity
Flourishing happily
Afrika free
The whole world
Should agree
It is it's
Entry
And our exit
Out into
What we should
Be

FULL GROWN TREE

The great tree
Planted in the 13th century
Growing strong
Growing fast and profound
From just a seed
A camp
A neighborhood
A town
A state
A country
A universal tree
Deeply rooted
Into solid ground
Leave forever green
Money green
Mankind beautiful the scene
Black and red
Afrika strong
Deeply rooted into the ground covered with earth
Fertilized
By blood and sweat
Keeping her colors
Bright
Her appearance
Profound
She shades
The whole wide world
Her flowers are yellow
And it blossoms
Year around
A big tree

Growing fast growing strong
Growing long
Profound
It's root goes
Deep

#1 HOUSE

King of the jungle
Lord of the pride
The conqueror of all
In the savanna
You can't hide
From the alpha lion
And the
Queen of the pride
In the savanna
They have never
Been denied
The king knows all
Through his wisdom
Scanner
The queen makes the call
And the lioness
Collects the manna
The young male
Protects the halls
Making sure no one
Crosses the banner
The respect
Have not yet fall
The pride is the wall
That houses the family
In the savanna

WHITE PONY

I'm back
On my pony again
I'm seeing things
On the scene
I'm jumping hills
I'm crossing streams
I'm riding beside
My Afrikan queen
The skies are so blue
The grass is green
I'm back
On my pony again
There is a rainbow
In the west
True
It colors
Lights up the nature scenes
To the east
There grows a garden green
Fresh water daily
From Heavenly rain
So now you see
I'm not feeling no pain
I'm back on my pony again
Again

NAKED EYES

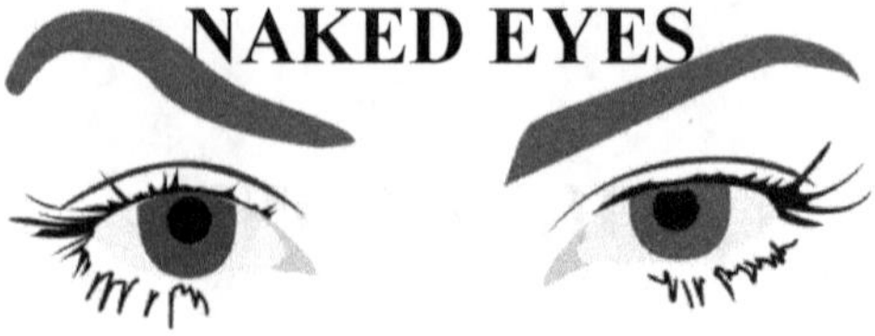

Watching the
Grass grow
Watching
The paint dry
Watching
The tide over flow
Watching
The willow tree cry
Watching
The light as it springs out
Watching
The flower live and die
Watching
The waves move about
You saw that
Watching
The wing blow by
Watching
The land dry drought
Watching
The sun right in the eye
Watching
The third crocks of doubt
Watching
The unseen multiply
Watching
The grass grow
Watching the future try

MY AFRIKA

In my Afrika
The people are
The most colorful in the world
From the city dwellers
To the tribe village
The most complete
Civilization on earth
They have everlasting gold
And great worth
Silver springs
Diamonds of curse
Forest forever living
Jungle full
With the cries of new birth
The great blue Nile
The traditional tribal styles
Continent of the wild
Living wild living free
Long time before
The white man entry
My Afrika
Is in the 13th century
When the leaders were black
Just like me
Now it is all black history
In my Afrika
I was free

LOVE RULES

A stream of water for the thirsty to day
A garden of fruit for the hungry
I pray
A beam of light
For the blind
To see their way
A grain of hope
So that the lame
Won't be lame to stay
An ear of faith
So that the deceased
Want to make earth pay
A seed of wisdom
So that the children
Can be happy to play
A pinch of knowledge
To end the wars
Remember
Brother blue brother gray
A bit of over-standing
So that our future can be relay
And a whole wide world of love
For all to worship love for all to
Obey
Water
For the thirsty
To day

BRAIN AND HAND

Man's hand
In the hands of the man
Handy man
Hand on man
A whole hand
Palm of the hand
Hands on
Hand to hand
A good hand
Hands off
Hands up
Hands behind your back
Hands down
Give me a hand
Don't put your hand
Hand stand
Hand gun bad hand
Need a hand
Watch your hand
Quick hand
Shaky hand
Out of hand
Steady hand
Hold my hand
Oh what a hand
Handsome

BE FREE

This one is for
The brothers
Locked
In the penitentiary
Brothers
Learn your time
Get yourself prepared
For when
You are free
Don't let it
Blow your mind
You have responsibilities
Come back
Stay in line
For your kids
You are family
But while you're waiting
Time
Be free
Visit the library
Dictionary
And when you feel
The grind
Always remember
Get down on your knees
When they threw
The signs
Always remember
How you use to be
Just leave it
Behind

Locked up
In the penitentiary
My brothers
Learn your time
One day
You will be free
Free mind

AWAY, AWAY

A dope a day
Keeps the mind away
No time to play
You find
You stay
You cry you pray
Crack back
The next day
Hitting away
Your dope a day
You're fine
Where you lay
When you can't pay
You whine all day
Get out of your way
Your mind
Won't say
You're fine
You pay
A dope a day
You smoke away
Your soul
I pray
U
B
Ok

A SPORT

Mind games
Her heart changes
In every scene
Gone in a glance
And then the same
Said she wants romance
But then
We never came
Said she
Wants to dance
But then
She stepped out
Shame
One minute
She's in a trance
And the next
She is perfectly sane
She takes
Your Franklin your Grants
And come to bed
With head pain
Let you take off your pants
Then she starts
Scrabbling the brain
Said she's going to France
Playing you
Vain
Tells you her wants
Her cant's
Then took off for Spain
With her love

You can't enhance
With your heart
She plays mind games
You've given her
Many chances
But situation
Still grows lame
She is a sport
She plays game

WHO'S WORLD (BABY)

Children all children
Each and every one
The seedling
Of our future
As we continue
To circle the sun
Secrets
Hidden
Inside of you
Grow strong grow smart
Let Jah
Will be done
The whole world will be
One day
Your world
For you to run
The old world
Will pass away
And the new will be put
To motion
So let the children play
Let them have
Joy and fun
Never turn them away
The future
We must survive
Abortion
Disease
The blood sheds
By the gun

In order for us
To save our selves
Our future must be
One
Won

TWO TO SIX A.M.

Can't think
Of me right now
My heart sinks
I wonder how
One blink
Mr. Wink
And all went sour
Too much to drink
Have unlock the power
Missing link
Three or four hours
Came home pink
Straight to the shower
Fell on the mink
She lift as a flower
What am i to think
I waited four hours
She fell asleep
In a blink
What am I to think
I can't think
Of you right now
Can't sleep a wink
My heart sank
I wonder how
Two 'til six a.m.

Way you been?

THE ROCK ROAD

E.Z. to love
Hard to follow
Faith up above
Down here it's hollow
White as a dove
But small
Like a sparrow
E.Z. to love
Out of his shadow
Say he is above
Sins have been swallow
Wings of a dove
Is your tomorrow
E.Z. to love
Hard to follow
The trails of a dove
The way
He has traveled
Needle narrow
You follow true love

REBILL$

Changes for the good
Changes for the bad
When you live
In the hood
Most of the changes
Are bad
Nothing new
Where the old stood
Cracked up streets
That drives you Mad
Half torn building
Held by rotted wood
Playground unrepaired
Looks so sad
The only changes
In the hood
Changes for the bad

CROSSES AND HEARTS

Crosses and heart
In which do you trust
Is your heart true
Do the crosses
That we wear
Make us true
Does it help
Will you cross your heart to it
Be real about it
My heart is true
My cross seals it
I cross my heart
To it

THE BOTTOM LINE

Warriors they are
On the ghetto
Front line
Paving the way
For the future leading mind
So they won't be
Stuck
In the ghetto grind
Sacrificing
A ghetto sacrifice
Making a way out
Out of the ghetto bind
Doing whatever it take
To get out of ghetto misery
To leave the ghetto far
Far behind
Selling drugs
And sometimes
Self
The quickest way out
Some find
Living in the bottoms streets
Hopeless
Is the street signs
Whenever is your time
You do what you gotta do
To keep a peace of mind
Sometimes abuse
The nine
Ghetto warriors
On the front line

Making the future
Better than the present time
Ghetto blinds

THE BILL PAYER

You play the games like trash
Too fast wo legs on the dash
Too quick you ask I cash
That love
Don't ever last
You share it like Steve Nash
Every balla you come pass
All you see is the math
'Drumertry is your class
You long for greener grass
Keep on your schema mask
You dis the Mrs.
Too fast
Not learning from your
Last pass
Your vanity
Is massive vast
You play the game dirty
Like trash
To quick
Legs on the dash
And now you want some
Cash?

TRUE HATE

I hate
Hatred
Hatred hates me
I hate I'm
With a passion
I hate its misery
I hate the way
Its fashioned
In the 21st century
I hate what
It does to love
And how it makes
It enemy
I hate everything about hate
From the word
To the very last vowel E
I hate
Hatred
For what hate wants to be
I hate
Hatred
And now I know
Hatred hates me

THE STUDENT

Hey Mr. cop, why did you shoot my brother down?
I know he did not do anything wrong
He was on his way to the Holy church
To pray and to sing a gospel song
What did he do that was so bad
To make you bring him down?
He never smoke or drink
All he ever did was read and think
Of what guilt has he ever been found?
He never sold drugs
He never hang with thugs
But in his head, there is your slugs
He always had a job
He never steal or rob
But he is lying dead on the ground
Why did you shoot my brother Officer?
Why did you shoot him down?
Just today, he was fitted for his diploma, cap, and gown
Why did you shoot my brother, cop?
What did he do so wrong?

SITUATIONAL RAPP

Situational rapp
Tells what it is
Situational rapp
Nobody's bizz
Educational rapp
All about the kids
Emotional rapp
About the slavery fizz
Sensational rapp
Put you in a dizz
Social rapp
Not hidden behind a gizz
Inspirational rapp
Mind yours and his
Temptational rapp
Talking to the Ms.
Spiritual rapp
Holy men over wizz
Situational rapp
Telling what it is
Situational rapp
Telling no one's bizz

BROTHER NATURE

Brothers all over our nation
To our dear sisters
We are an inspiration
A godly figure
The manly motivation
On daily bases
There should be a celebration
For the gift she's given you
Grows on through generation
The genes and all the right things
We should do
Carry on past graduations
To self we must be true
A leader in your congregation
A job we must
Always pursuit
If another
Is in cancellation
Always remember our roots
Keep brotherly love
Incorporated
Then sisterly love
Will grow and show
For me and you
All over the nation
Acceleration

BILL CHECK

I'm just done
Checking my bills
And it has me
Feeling
Kind of ill
I'm writing this poem
From my sill
I dear not
Take a pill
I have yet
To write my will
I'm just held up
By this sea of bill
There
Taking me to the mill
On the chains
Of negative thrill
Bills
By bill by bill
All piled up
On an unpaid hill
On its way
To the nearest land fill
I can't
Check
My bills

1 PLUS 2 PLUS 3

High up on the X
You have lost
Your whole aspect
You have cross the line
What's next
It gives you mind
Defect
In a matter of time
You're wreck
Caught up onto
Three four five X
Educated fools
Science project
It will make you uncool
A reject
Sex
You will break your own rules
Lose respect
Act very cruel
Personality effect
Don't jump into the cesspool
X will direct
You're perfect
Turn you into ghoul
It's like X
Put them in a hex
Don't cross out your life
With X

TEMP FEARS

There is this fear
Who's name is temptation
It will get
Into your brain
And complicate
Your relation
Move in to your heart
And in a bad situation
And if you fall
For it
You could end up
In fornication
And from that day on
Your love will be
Mixed up exaggeration
That leads into
Untrust
A break down in motivation
If you overcome the fear
Of that bully
They calls the temptation
You will move
Into the lights
Of true love
And many celebration
And in the times ahead
Rice throwing
Congratulation
And soon all will be love
A most romantic
And ever lasting

Honeymoon vacation
Love conquer all
Big bad temptation

EIGHTEEN YEARS HARD TIME

I slept with this lady
I love her so
Mess around and had a baby
I wasn't sure if I was ready for the changes
But I had to go eighteen years hard time
and if she does good; even more
Man I had to get on my grind
Keeping her fed and dress
From her head down to her toes
Working on a five to nine
Making sure she gets the best
And letting my love truly show
Down here doing hard time
Taking care of mind
You gotta go
You gotta go
Eighteen years
'Cuz baby is mine
The DNA is good to go
My baby girl is feeling fine
Judge said eighteen years and maybe more
Nine to five or five to nine
Do the right time
Let her know

UNWANTED

A queen
Will want me
But will I want
A queen
The scene will want me
Will I take
The scene
The lane's gonna want me
Will I shake the lane
The fiends will want me
How can I escape a fiend
The dream gonna want me
How will I wake
From the dream
The pain
Will want me
What will I take
For the pain
The game wants me
I've already taken
The games
The big screen will want me
How will I pre-pose
The screen
The green's gonna want me
Blood tests
High-dro green
The brains will want me
Run test on me
My brain
The reign

Gonna want me
Because I'm a king
In this wanted game
But
How will I shake the queen

TWO WAY LADDER

My days are getting happier
My nights are getting
Sadder
I'm climbing
In this world much higher
But love keeps falling shorter
Conquering my love
Life dream desires
Love nightmares
It doesn't matter
All day my life
On fire
At night it is the ladder
In the morning
On the high wires
Dawn and dust
Thinking
When I had her
My days are getting
Sadder
The same ladder
Bringing me up
In to success
Bring me down on love
Climb it with me
My love
At night
I cannot get no rest

TEACHER

I think I have a thing for my teacher
In the shower songs I sing of teacher
In the classroom my eyes cling
To teacher the sweetest apple
I will bring the teacher
Above her head there floats a ring
I'll reach her
Deep in side
I have this thing
For teacher
A lesson from up above
My teacher
Got me floating like a dove
To reach her
Fitting the teacher
Like a glove
I've breach her
I think my heart have fallen
In love
A preacher
I'm very, very fortunate of
My teacher
I'm keeping it under cov—
I'll reach her
Graduating school in love
With teacher I think I have a thing

MICROFINE GLASS

From a microfine street
Blown up into millions
Fine wine in your glass
At the table largest chair
Signing autograph
The player of the year
Living life divine
Dining first class
Top of the line
Under a microfine glass
Knowing your everywhere
Player, keep it in line
In bound with the pass
From a microfine street
A very big eye peeps
From the small end
Of a microfine glass
Making sure you behave
White class waiting so, for you to repeat the past
Don't file out or get kick out
Don't drive your cars too fast
Make too much pass
Smoke too much grass
Give your cheerleaders
Too much cash and don't shoot up'
Your timing in the 20 yard dash
Doping
Keep yourself in the clear
So we can see you
From a microfine glass
And not from

A microfine street
You could be the last

MANNA ON THE MENU

Manna's on the menu
Food for thought
The righteous meal
To take away
The sins out you
Fill you up
With the good and smart
It is only for
Who is truly true
A daily prayer
Living the part
It shines the heart
With a high glow
The baking
Of nature's greatest chef art
For the starving souls
Eats it slow
When your last supper
Is manna
Your eternal life starts

IN THE PROOF

Hey black berry, how sweet is your juice
So fine, you're scary
Got us on the goose
Feeling all weary
Trying to break it loose
That tail deer, is like a fairy
I'm harking like a moose
Tall, dark, and real hair
I see
I wonder if she's deuce
She like ‘em
Slim like soldier Larry
Or thick like Bruce, Pruce
Hey there black berry
Portent is your juice
Fine and thin
Like Halle berry
No Don Perry
Hooking us to the goose
It's not about the cherry
It's the drink that get you loose
Fine just like a fairy, but it's all about
The sweetest juice and black
Is the sweetest berry of all
Taste it in the juice
100% juice

FREEWAY

You do your thing in the day
And play with minds at night
If you don't get your way
You just fuss we fight
Now you want to play
Let us do the thing right
You stay out of my way
I keep
Out of your sight
The game is over O.K.
I think I've got it right
You go on, you play
But don't be using me
For fights
My time
I have paid
Now
Things are looking bright
I counted my days
You hunted my nights
Now I'm on my way
Taking back my might
Out of your way
Taking back my life
I love you O.K.
But you're too forsaken
For a wife
You do your thing
By day
The free way

EIGHT HOT HOURS HOT

A summer
Nine to five
On a construction crew
Looking like
You've taken a dive
Your body soaking
Dew
Drinking one
Gallon of water
Sweating off two
Time is money
You've got to work
The whole day through
Lunch time comes
You don't jive
Get your rest
For the next four hours
You're in a fight
Call staying a live
A sunny nine to five
Labor
On a construction crew
In the evening
You wonder
In the morning
Can you be bribe
Sunburnt
Back aches
Wet up
Undo

I dream at night
Of an inside crew
Summer nine to five

AROUND BACK

Our hands
Are tied behind our back
We can see
But cannot help
Our own people under attack
The coke
The heroin
The X'es on crack
Our hands are tied
So we don't look back
The police
The jailer
The judge the lawyer
All running with the pack
We just honor
And don't look back
The employer
The employee
The land lord
The trustee
They all just want to see you
Lack
But we just turn
And walk right back
The teacher
The doctor
The grower
The preacher
They're all up in front
Only for what
They can get back

Our hands are tied
And around our back
We tied then there
By not looking back

WINNER ON THE STREET

On my street I'm discrete
Never been defeat
Never tote heat
All I meet
A positive greet
With love
I treat
Respected
By the meek
On the worst bad corner
On the worst cold street
Even pistol Pete
Throws it down
When we meet
My faith is indiscrete
I've never been defeat
Comfortable and neat
When I hit my street
The whole damn city speak
No one here a freak
All differently meek
That is why
I always greet
Focus when we meet
Where one indiscrete

I’ve never been defeat
Never tote heat
On my street
Indiscrete

UNSTABLE TABLE

Every day
Living has got
To be earned
No one out there
Giving
You have got to make
The table turn
Determination
Success driven
Use all
Of what you learn
Good
Stay in school
Be concern
Stand up
And the table turns

TWINS

Caught up
In a yoke
Our necks are tied
Your throat
My stroke
From you
I can’t hide
When you choke i choke

One rule we abide
Two laughs one joke
When you slip
I slides
I get high when you tokes
Together one pride
You eats hog
I gets pork
Forever world wide
I suffocate
In your smoke
To you
I can't lie
My pockets empty your broke
Side by side
Brother to brother
Where folk

THREE LIGHTS

I couldn't sleep
Last night
I tossed and turn
I kept seeing these lights
Couldn't figure out
Lying down sleeping tight
What was going on'
Until I raised up
And started to write
These new sounds
It came to me
And I started to see
That dream was to be
My plight

To help the poor
Get right
In the slums and ghettos
Get the soldiers ready
Tight
For the Armageddon fight
Teach the children
How to honor respect
And to stand up
For their rights
To give thanks and praise to Selassie I
The trinity
Was that light
Hold tight

THE VISIONS OF MR. TELLY

Tele
Tells every thing
Catch your vision
Tells you thing
Every thing
Chose a channel
And tone in
TV speaks
TV sings
Send signals
Whispering
Everything
Instant winter
Switch on spring
Tone it on and a bling
Hit the volume
And it sing

Every body's business rings
Queen kings
Can I get a witness
Every damn thing
Tele on the stars
Where they've been
Who they do
Where they hang
Then change the station
And you can tell
Who's acting
TV tells every thing
Telly tells vision
Tele tells dreams
Tele tells religion
Tele tells schemes
Telly tells
How big
Is the diamond ring
Tele tells who's
Got a thing
Tele tells vision
Make your ear ring
But one thing
Tele don't tell
The whole truth
About anything
Just acting

THE OTHER WAY

The whole
World is hurting
With Babylon
They're flirting
Behind closed skirting
The true word of god
Peace

BE YOU

The more you know
The more you show
The more you see
The more you be
The more you hear
The more you care
The more you feel
The more you reveal
The more you do
The more comes true
Just be you
Yours…

THE BABIES KNOW

Daddy
Don't do no more
Too much bugs
Coming in the door
Daddy
Don't do no more
Remember
What you said before
That you weren't
Going to do no more
It takes you fast
And makes you slow
And the next day
Feeling low
Wondering
How you can even up
The score
Losing everything
That you had was pure
Daddy
Don't do no more
When weakness calls
Please don't go
Because when it starts
All shows
Your eyes glow
You don't know
Broken hearts
Hard like ice
Cold as snow
You rain insane and it pours

Let bugs in the doors
Papa
Please don't do no more

SUCCEED YOU

Mama your daughters need you
Show your daughters
How to please you
Show your daughters
How to succeed you
Show your daughters
How to read you
Show your daughters
How to lead true
Mama your daughters
Need you
Show your daughters
How to plead through
Show your daughters
How to heed you
Show your daughters
How the seed grew
Show your daughters
How to feed you
Show your daughters
What the weed does
Mama your daughters
Need you
Tell her to let the breed through
Mama your daughters
Succeeds you

SOUND BLOOD

Young blood
Strong blood
Freedom is in
The sound blood
Be profound blood
Spread it around blood
Keep it brown blood
Sing your song blood
Burn the pound blood
Take the mound blood
Hang in there long blood
Don't you drown blood
Watch them hound blood
Don't you frown blood
Take it like
Kong blood
Top of the town blood
Play the ground blood
Wear the crown blood
It's thicker than water
Blood

PRISON

Situation is
Out of control
Everyday
More and more black men enroll
Leaving black women behind
Paying the toll
Family crying brother got time
Being dragged away
Vision of days
When brother was sold
But now
Lock away in a prison hole
He took a chance
Went for the gold
Took more than
A glance
Brother got bold
Heard the word in
Advance
Brother didn't fold
Same player lost his pant
Now that player
Done gone to France
Who hung that player
Up on that pole
Now the cop got me
In the stance
On my way down
To the hole
Situation
Out of control

OVER KILL

Crack kills
Smack ills
Don't get your kicks
Taking pills
The first hit
Is a thrill
Your last bit
Makes you fit
Takes your bills
Needle traces blood spilled
All ways empty
Can't be fulfilled
Blind can't see
You have cross the sill
Can't hear the trill
Talking through
A cracked up grill
Wake up every day
And go through the same old drill
Over kill

MOLD AND CHIP

Dear little sister
The mold of our mother
With love
From your brother
The chip of our father
You are
Peace
In my heart

For ever
To me
Like none other
We have always been
Good
Dear to one another
Sister you inspired me
You're all grown up now
With your own family
Remembering
As kids
How time used to be
The times we had
The time we play
We pray
When we were one
Close family
Funny
How time have pass away
Now it is all
A cherish memory
Sister for ever
I will be like you
You will be
Just like me
Let us stay true
True to each other
My sister
Your brother
Me and you
We be true

LOVE YOU

It's all about
Respect
Having your own
Aspect
Keeping your self
Connect
With your self
Should never be reject
Love and embrace
What your manners
Reflect
It is what you
Feeds
Teaches and protect
It is you first
You elect
It is you first
You keep in check
What you are
Is what you
Reflect
It is all
A matter of respect

I HOPE

Deep in my heart
I know
I care
Of all the things
I see
That I am aware
Of all the people
Are living under fear
And all of the places
Through war
Put in despair
Like living in the ghetto
A million people
Living in a one ¼ mile square
Wrapped
In a criminal blanket
No light no care
No fresh water or air
Where problems
And not solution
Always seems to flare
Sometimes here
Sometimes there
Most of the time
Every where
Living in a life
Without glare
Only seeing life
Always from the rear
Police brutality gets in your hair
Ghetto misery

There's no compare
Deep in my heart

I BE YOU BE

Treat me like a king
I'll give you
Everything
Royalty
I will bring
Heavy diamond ring
You will be my bling
Love letters
And
I will sing
Love songs in the spring
To my honey
Sweet thing
Just
Treat me like a king
I want the whole thing
The sweet songs
You sing
When we let it hang
That fresh fragrance
Spring
That makes me wants
To cling
Those kisses
Gives me wings
I want the whole thing
I'll give you

Everything
My love and my ring
My heart on a string
My mind
And my bling
My body
Everything
Just treat me like a king
And queen
I will be
Your king

HANGERS

Eyes wide open
Wanting
Everything
Looking and hoping
Around the streets you hang
Peeping and scoping
Trying to find a yang
Falsely cooping
Like a puppet on a string
Always loping
Until you see a sting
You're just snooping
Trouble that you bring
Eyes wide open
Scoping everything
Broken, you're hoping
Around the streets
You cling

FRIENDSHIP

Sailing free
Sailing happily
Sailing without envy
No room on this ship
For jealousy
It is your waves
That is important to me
Throw me a line
I won't lie
You down
Come in
When you come in
Go out
When you go out
Fish high tide
Or fish low tide
Or fish deep sea
I don't need to know
Come in two or three
It's alright with me
This ship we sail
Is free
Sailing happily
Sailing without envy
There is no room
For jealousy
Friendship sailing free

FISHING MEN MISSION WOMEN

Come on boy
Let's go fishing
Come one girl
On this mission
Ship ahoy
Let's go fishing
The catch of joy
Let's go fishing
Bring the boys
Out of hell's kitchen
Drop the toys
Let's go fishing
Girls ship ahoy
Stop that wishing
Drop the toys
Let's go fishing
Girls and boys
A faithful mission
A world of joy
Let's go fishing

FATHER

Man
You are the one
Man
You are the light
You protect your daughter
And sons
To your wife
You are the light
You provide
For every one
In battle
You lead the fight
Man
You are the one
Your ways should be
Upright
In every rising
Of the morning sun
Give thanks
Before you lie down
At night
Man
You are the father
You are the light
The one
Man

DADDY WAY-OR

All alone
In a world
Full of predators and prey
The teenage thrill is gone
Now
I've got to pave my way
The man in me
Have dawn
Daddy way-or
I took the high way
To pay the price
A man pay
Gathering up my life
Start building for
My day
Looking for my wife
The truth
For i to pray
On my way
A man
All alone now
With only Jah
For I to obey
I took the highway
The world
In mine

BREAD WINNER

1o1
They say
It would be
A hot sun
Today
Out there waiting
For me
But man
I've got to run
Go get that salary
Life is not much fun
Working so hard
For such
A small fee
What you've gotta do
Got to be done
When you are the man
Father of the family
You are the one
Who breaks the bun
Mother daughter son
All depends
On my stability
1o1
In the shade
Not in the sun
Happily

BOY TOO BAD

Mama told me
Son
Don't be too bad boy
Grow in to a man
Drop
Your childish toys
You have got to
Overstand
This world
Is not a joy
It is about
Keeping food for the pans
Keeping your self
Employed
Not depending
On giving hands
Not letting
Your self-destroy
Not joining
The alley band
And not hanging
With any old Roy
Or sleeping
With just any new fan
Son, life is the real McCoy
She said to put away my childish toys
Take life serious and enjoy
Jah is with you son
Don't be too bad boy
Mama knew

BLACK STYLE

Black and style
Kool
Sometimes wild
I like to see
When them
Beautiful black lady's smiles
With the lip stick on
Of her black style
Because she's dark
Like the ladies
Of the Nile
She is a different
Flower
Her color has power
Like a fragrance
That stays
In your mind
Arouse your fantasy
And keeps it there
For a while
You know that
Fine
I'm talking about
The one that stays
In your head
Under the girl most wanted
Files
Every time you glance
Her figures
It turns you
To stare

She drives you
Afrikan wild
That skin that hair
Pure beauty
So rear
There's nothing
To compare
The power of black beauty
Lingers in the mind
The truth
Is in the stare
When seen from afar
Can't wait
To see near
Better when she passes by
Your eyes lurks
And you know where
So don't run around
Acting so
She is rear
Like you don't stare
Or you don't know
Or not aware
Those beautiful black ladies
Are the most
Fairest
Of them all
To them there
Is no compare

BEEN AROUND

I'm gonna pack my shit
I'm gonna leave this town
I won't look back
I won't turn around
Looking for my future
Where there
It can be found
A new atmosphere
There where I will be bound
Looking around for a place
One sound to reveal
My lyrical rapps my songs
Put my legend on the map
A star
Budding ground
Wedging up
Not looking down
No cap until
I make the crown
I'm through
With all that
Weighting
Around
The dogs and the pounds
Finish with
The ballas bait
Leaving it
All in town
Looking for
Mind straight
Word power
Brand new town

Hear my words
Brand new songs
Down
Been around

BACK STREET

These streets are so ruff
I'm not lying
You've got to be tuff
Are you dying
When you've had enough heat
There is no crying
Streets full of ruff buff
And they are not trying
When you're in their cuff
There is no denying
There's just not enough
We're far; way behind
Things keep getting tough
Few turn to wine
Time is getting rough
Many doing time
Some huff and some puff
You know that line
These streets are so ruff
I am not lying
You've got to be so tuff
Are you dying
We can't get enough
We are so far behind
No crying

AS I AM

You can't see my real
Know not what I feel
Wonders what
Is my deal
If I'm one to squeal
Will I be hell on wheel
Will I tell on the deals
Am I packing steel
If my lips are seal
Who can make me kneel
Slick like an eel
I'm just keeping it real

A SOLID HOUSE

Intelligences
Soft
Quiet
Simple
Fair
Kind
Important
Loving
Care
Smart
Attractive
Wisdom
Aware
Trying
Perfective
True
Sincere
36
24
36
Around the rear

UNBABEL

The only ones in the universe
Is the ones of the sun
It is the only matter
Without compare
Of which everything is in conjunction
The light of the universe
To all light
It is the first
Giveth free its powerful gift
In equal shares to every planet
And to every living one recognizes
All over the earth
The same
We all calls light
The sun
Where ever he is
It is always day
His work is never done
Through the stars
Through the moon
He shines
Darkness
Has never won
How can there be
Two different god
When our true light
Is only one
Someone would have to be a fraud
Because our lights
Come from the one sun
And David is our father

He rays
Selassie I is the one
Unbabel

THE POOR BLESSING

800 million hungry
Ethiopians
Foodless on this earth
The pain begins at birth
Never ending
And growing
Getting worst
No doctor or nurse
No help
For the suffering souls
No diamond silver or gold
No oil and or charcoal
Nothing but poor souls
Starving
In the sight
Of a very rich world
Where the diseases
Of the heart
Is cold
Hearts that only
Give help
To friends and neighbors
Of gold oil control
800 million hungry
In the world
8 million rich
In the world

Together
Eyes can see light
Through the eye
Of a needle
May Jah Bless their souls

DIRTY LIKE A FOX

Slick like a fox
Scheming for them rox
Where is your thinking box
All tear down
To your sox
Make you look
Like you're intox
Like you need
A hit--- Clorox
A little bit Borox
But you're full of shit
You know
And you won't admit your lock
And you won't quit
More rox
Makes you spit
And hide can't talk
Slick
Just like a fox
My tears drip down
To my sox
A whip
Is in the rock

CAT TALK

Hot dog
Cats have nine lives
Curiosity kills the cat
But every dog has a day
When the cow jump over the moon
Oh you dirty rat
Lower than a snake belly
The heart of a lion
Slicker than a fox
Memory of an elephant
Birds eye view
Greedy like a pig
You hogs up everything
Hey is for horses
Monkey see monkey do
This is gator bait
Slicker than eel shit
The eyes of an eagle
If you're froggy leap
Junk yard dog
Hungry like a wolf
Wings of a dove
You dumb bird
Wearing tiger stripes
Ground hog day
The birds and the bees
Bear hugs
Runs like a rabbit
You chicken
If it quacks it's a duck
Bulls eye

Buffalo soldier
The lion from the tribe of Judah

13 DEGREES

13 degrees
Windchill at three
Working today
Is going to be
A cold and misery
We will pay today
For that salary
Eight hours today
Every day until Friday
It is going to be
Freezing every day
But money is needed
And work to be done
Sooner or later
It will be the hot sun
Six 30 in the morning
I have to run
Boot hat coat
A kiss from my Hun
It is going to be a very cold one today
13 degrees wind chill one
I wish there was a better way
But it is ok with daddy because my family
Keeps me warm happily working at zero degree

IN STRIVE

Cooking in the sun all day
On that nine to five
Hard working
Straight
Getting the pay
Keeping my hopes alive
No break or breeze ever comes this way
Everything moving in strive
Cloud rolling by but it never stays
And that sun there ain't no jive
In ninety nine degree
All day, no play
Making just enough to stay alive
Working in this heat
You pay
No break or breeze until after five
Bills moving fast
Money in strive
Sun hurry past
Nine to five
Pay won't last
Cooking alive

UPON A STAR

The skies are full
With mysterious lights
You don't know
Which are stars
You glance
Into the night
You see
A blinking light
You wonder
Is that a star
Then you lose its sight
Was that just
An airplane
Passing through in flight
Or maybe
It's a falling star
A meteorite
On the other side
Of the darken sky
You see a light that glides
Could it be a star
Maybe it is
An unidentified object
Or a planet way out far
And we can only see them
As the light
Of a tiny star
Then I look
Afar
Into the other direction
Could that be a star

Or is it just
A satellite
Or a gun
We use for war
Maybe one of them rocks
That scientist call quasar
The skies are full
So many lights
I wonder upon
A star

TO BE

The sweetest thing
You've ever known
Walk into my life
Or was she flown
To be my potential wife
Fine and grown
It was baked
And already to slice
With all of her own
The cake have met the knife
Two perfectly born
To be
In just one life
One love on and on
To be
Husband and wife
Or to be

SUGAR AND ICE

You've got so much sweetness
Sweetie, you're just like cotton candy combined
With your good taste
You should be renamed spice
Every time I see your face something always make me look twice
It is just like that;
Da ja voo
As if you have entice some kind of magical device
Taking control of sensation
You holds it up so nice
Just one smile that special look
Puts a man up there under the spells
Rendering him unwell
Blocked off like hell
From any good advice he hears
What she want him to hear
While he pays the total price
Not ever hitting any points
Like rolling from the six
Fix side of the dice
But still thinking
One day some way
You and her could walk
The sacred line
Under the sacred
Rain of rice
Because she is so sweet
So nice
But some time
Bitter is the taste in spice
and sage comes fine and crystal
But some time hard as ice

RIDING HOOD

Sister, sister
Your heart is so good
Sister
Trapped in the hood
Sister
Looking so good
Sister
Miss understood
Sister, sister
Black beauty hidden under hoods
Sister
Lost in the woods
Sister
If it can be done
Sister could
Sister
What needs to be done
Sister would
Sister
Heart's so good
Sister
A flower in the hood
Woods
Sister, sister
Love so good
Sister
Looking for Mr. Good
Sister
Miss understood
Sister

Black riding hood
Sister
Lost in the hood
Sister knows
Players never could
Sister knows
Players never would
Sister, sister
Mrs. Understood

CONGRATULATIONS

Graduation day
The end
Of the start
set out on the way
The world stage
To play
Your life live
Part
Everything came
Out from clay
Molded into art
Out to get
Life's pay
Congratulation
You have made the
Finish chart
Start
On the right path
To hope
You stay
That diploma
Yearly very smart
Remember
Always pray
Always let
The right way
Always lead
Direct
Your educated heart
The start

BAD CALL

My baby mama called
Said she wanted to meet me at the mall
Said her already weak;
Week salary have already (fall)
And she have been doing it all
Little girl needs a new baby doll
An my son needs some basic balls
She needs some brand new walls
And I need a U-haul
The bad call

WISDOM

Knowledge and overstanding
Patience
And nondemanding
Aged smarts
Experience heart
Seen many things finish
Seen many things start
Seen many depart
Time adds up
Into years
Grows up
And lose your fears
A survivor
You have more heart
You cares
In the struggle
More respect
Surviving pairs

You sometimes count
As time grows near
Your eyes don't see as well
But your visions are much clearer
Life moves on faster
More time to put to prayer
Wisdom is full of tears

OLD SCHOOL

Old school new rule
Remember when
School was cool
Kick ball and monkey bars
Back then student didn't drive cars
Soft ball dodge ball
Player didn't hang out in the hall
Hide and seek
Merry go around
We use to smile
Then
Not just frown
Bingo and playing spade
The strongest drink then
Was lemonade Kool aid
Go stand in that corner
Or the teachers strap
No one had to worry
If a student snap
Remember when
The lunch bell rang
And everyone rush
To play in the swing
Those were the days when school was cool
We all learned our best
And followed the school rule
Didn't went just to dress
And thought
We had our parent
Fooled
Cool days

4 MAN 1 GOD

Haile Selassie
Earth rightful ruler
Near and far
He said until the philosophy
That holds one race inferior
And another superior
Is abandoned
There will be war

Marcus Garvey
Man of mobility
He said up you mighty race
Be proud black is beautiful
You're from Afrika
Great is your history

Martin King
Man with the great dream
He said from every mountain
And through every stream
Let freedom ring
For all the races
One the same

Malcolm X
Prophet whom came
From the streets
He said at any means necessary
We must earn our own
Protect our own

And greet every man
On our feet

Nesta Marley
Rasta man
Who sang the true words
To me
He said get up stand up
And fight for your rights
Our god name is
Haile Selassie I

225TH

They think the king is dead
But he's very much alive
They all have been misled
Some have even been bribed
Don't let dem
Get in your head
Dem all are Jekyll and Hyde
They didn't get it
What the Bible said
And their hearts
Are filled with jive
They didn't believe
Our blood was even red
Out of ten virgin
True was five
So keep close watch
Of whom you break bread
And hold fast to faith
Until the king arrive
He will be coming
From the tribe of Judah

We must be
On the road to victory
We must be strong
To bare the sea
And prepare our selves
For the wipe daily
Be able to sleep in chains
Above our shoulders
And below our knees

On the road to victory
We must be ready to hear the cries
Of our women and our innocent babies
Ready to say goodbye to our home land country
Ready to sleep in piles of our own
Flesh and body
We must be on the road to victory
Ready to eat the rotted food
To secure our destiny
Keep the kool
As we sail
Back
Across the open sea
On our way back to Afrika
Away from where
We was when we were
In slavery

TREASURE

I once was
An American slave
Down in the South Carolinas
Now I am a black man
Whom have found
His own faith
Now I am waiting
On the Blackstar liner
I heard she'll be coming
From the east
On to the west California
Picking up all
Whom heart is good
Taking them all back yonder
To the land
From whence we came
Long ago Afrika
Before the White man
Found her Treasure

TIED UP

My life is
All day long
Being tested
Nights and days
Brothers
Arrested
It seems our souls

Are being messed with
Something we don't have
Being requested
Something we did not do
Is being broadcasted
Seems the whole world
Is infested
No one wants to stand up
And confess it
Just keeping all in
Just digest it
Until the end
You poor damn bastard

THE ONLY THING

My whole life
I wanted to be something
Because I am afraid of ending up
Being nothing
I sometime feels
That I should have everything
To share with them
Whom don't have anything
Especially the truth
To them whom chosen
Another thing
That is in the world
There's only one thing
Praise Jah
And life will be
A fun thing

STILL RUNNING

Dear Afrika
My Dear native continent
My home
I have been gone
For so very long
But i have not yet forgotten you
Ever since the day i left
I have been trying
To get back to you
The men that took us
Are very smart
But in their world
Most of the people
Have very cold hearts
They have been doing every thing
In the powers
Of guns and fear
To keep us here
To hold up the bottom part
Fighting in fights
That someone who hates
Us starts
No equal right
It has been four hundred years
Since we've depart
Now I write back home to you
That for four hundred years
You still have my
Heart Afrika love
Doing my part

SHACKLED TOGETHER

The doors are open
For us to be free
When will we
Stand up
Together to be free
Togetherness
Is our keys
The only way for us to be
Free
Together we arrived in slavery
Equally
And only together
We are the keys
As one people together
We are the keys
As one people together
Blossom into prosperity
One before the other
Is not out history
We were all equally
Put into slavery
Now only together
Can we all be totally free
Together we fall
Into slavery
Together we rise
And let all be free
The doors are open
For us to be free
When we band together
And let us be free

RESERVATION

America reservation

The land is the people's and the people

Is the Indian nation

Wherever the people go

So be their country

They were here before

The Plymouth rock entry

Came knocking at their shores

Claiming America is our country

Indians are the real American

If you know our history

Everyone else is slash American

Let's see the Americans free

American preservation

MASSA DISASTER

Yes sir Massa
No sir Massa
I know Massa your disaster
Slave trading pasture
Jesus love broadcaster
For given in the after
Just grows your
Hate more faster
Justify disaster
Tell us
You are the after
Make our men
Out bastard
Have your own son
Being mastered
Control by guns and caskets
Every night
The daughters are trashed
Putting mother and son
In the same basket
So cold our soul
Was harassed
Whipped
For four hundred years
Like we were
Made of plastic
Tried to break us
With fear
Now you think
We are just here for
Gymnastics
Yes sir master
No sire master
We know master
You're disasters

JJ WHITE

This is a story
Of the brothers of the corn
One name Jim
And the other name john
Hated black people
From the day they were born
Two of the most notorious killers
Since the day
The first American night dawn
Set out to terrorize
And scorn
Jim was a murderer
Of black human rights
And john was a slayer
That road through the night
Together they prey
Upon blacks
And all non-white
Became heroes among
Masters
And that
History was kept
Out of sight
Brothers of the corn
Your heir have harvest
The killing goes on
May Jah forgive you
Buckro Jim
And brother john

GRAND THEFT

My past was stolen
By the white man
For four hundred years
He robbed
My poor grand
Of our wealth
And pride
All the work of their hands
Used up
To make rich
The plantations
The white man
Kidnapped and taken
From the mother land
Brought here and held
Four hundred years
Ransom demand
High seas robbery
Piracy
Was their wicked plan
Build the new country
Using up
The black man
But he is stolen property
But he is on American land
What will we tell the judge
When we are called
To the stand
He was 3/5 man

GET UP

Get up
No one wants to
Stand up
For what is right today
As long as
It don't effect you
That means it's ok
No one saw me
Maybe I might get away
They have every thing
We have nothing
Maybe we should
Make them pay
We have every thing
They have nothing
It is their fault
They live that way
In the church
The preacher purse
To certain things the bible says
In the street the police flaws
And sometime
Under the street
Table pays
In the house they represent
Lies
To protect his rep
For election day
The teacher teach
The one that can be reach
The bad apples are directed away
Visit the doctor

Without insurance
They won't be happy to see you
Don't want you to stay
Go see a lawyer
He will be happy to see you
But boy you better pray
Go to the bank
To borrow some money they will pay you no attention
But lend you
Directions
On your way
No one wants to stand up
For poor, poor people today
There is no way

DE-LYNCH

A message
To all the families
Whom are
Ex-owners of ex-slaves
Whom received
And carried out
The teaching
That their master
Willy lynch gave
In the future
You should try to change things
Because of the thing
Your parents changed
In the past
They have done the work
Of the haters
Four hundred years
That work have last
And you gave no help
To my people
You're people stole
We build this country
Solid as gold
Now you are telling us
Our stories are old
Yes lynch
Your plans was bold
My people is left
In a state of babel
Separated unfold
All mixed up in your

Slave games
Of scrabble
Not knowing where from
We came
And not knowing to where
We're going
Not knowing
We are
Still Afrikan and for Afrika
Our true love
Must truly show
In order to break
The mental chains
Of brutality and slavery
Free our minds
And seek to learn
What all Afrikan should be
And should know
Our past is the greatest
Grand
The first written history
And upon this
Our future
As a whole will grow
From this hole
We must not let lynch hate
Control us willy lynch was a hater!
And we all know
From and to whence all haters go
To all his followers
Time is up
And I thought
Y'all should know
Willy lynch is waiting for you

In a fires
Down below
It is no longer worth
Our
Wait in gold

COOL USER

On the first day
We arrived in America
We have been
Used up as a tool
To build this great country
We were treated
Just like mule
With no rights and no laws
For us they had their own rules
We became properties
Of soul losers
That did not learn
Love justice
And equality in their schools
Can you imagine
Right this day
Being controlled
By an uneducated fool
Just the way
The merciless dealers
Are doing our families in the hood
An ungodly situation
Cool users
Not so cool

BROKEN PEOPLE

Is this that
You have mouth on me
Or you just have
So much doubt in me
Does someone have
Us fixed
Are we the victim
Of someone's dirty tricks
Maybe it's just the gods
We pick
We just might have
Some root on us
Is someone tampering
With the fruit tree
I have heard about
That mojo
The kind
That takes your mind
And puts you in the
Slow mo'
For the things you know
I think sometimes
We might be curse
The way that things
Are going now
It has got to be reversed
Or we will be damn
Who is uncle tom

BLACK AFRIKA

You tried
To eliminate our race
Found out it couldn't be done
So you built
A real big gun
And flew off into space
To cut us off
Up there
Babylon your missions
A waste
We cannot be stopped
By your spaced race
No matter what judge
Handles the case
We are the alpha
And will be the omega
Of the whole earth human race
From the beginning
Onto the end
We controls home base
To the mansions
From the tent huts and dens
This is our father's place
Afrikan black men

I AM AN AFRIKAN MAN

I am an Afrikan man
Born in America
Raised in America
But still
An Afrikan man
They teach me
In their schools
They teach me
All their rules
Some I will never begin
To understand
Maybe that is
I am still an Afrikan man
Locked me in their jails
Because I am
A young black male
He said I didn't ran
That I belongs in a can
I don't think so that
I am still an Afrikan man
I guess my next stages would be
On my way back home
I hope to see
I get there soon
Before the bride
Meets the groom
Because in this red man's country
I feel my soul is doom
Slavery time is done
And they didn't break
Us all

All didn't run
I hope I am not the only one
To take that stand
To go back home to Afrika
The mother land
To our greatest great grand
Because deep down inside
Every one of us
Their lives
An Afrikan man

3473 MILES

The great blue Nile
A river bringing forth
Knowledge
Wisdom and style
Out of the mountains
Of Ethiopia
Flowing down through
Afrika
For over 3473 miles
Breaking drought
On its route
To water and feed
The civil and the wild
Over flows
And opens doors
Reaching the sad land
To breach a smile
Oh how giving
The great blue river
Nile
Pure is your start
On your journey through
The wild
Deliverance is your part
In your Ethiopian style
Over flow
And set free
Oh great blue river Nile

SIX- HUNDRED AND SOMETHING DAY

Hey Babylon
Your days are numbered
Won't be long
Before the days of thunder
The times
Hear
That made the old prophets
Wonder
Return
Noah, Moses Jesus, Muhammad
Help us please
Before we fall
Go down
Under
Burning lakes of fire
Receive that wicked number
Be doom
Within the sins
For the wicked days
We plunder
Voices will be heard
In the wind
Around the sound of thunder
Saying the same old things
Have been said
That will make
The new prophets
Wonder
The time of hade
Is above and under
Hey Babylon your great
Your days are numbered

BLACK SUPERMAN

Superman, Batman, Aquaman
Silverman, Goldman
Her-man he-man
Super heroes understand
But never did
A damn thing for human
Flies to the scene on our TV screen
Cut up looking lean like a super being
But it's all just a dream
A superman scheme
To mess up with our brain
Don't throw money
Down that drain
Super is Malcolm X
He stand against what was wrong
Super is Martin King
He stand for what was right
Super is Marcus Garvey
The Jamaican royal knight
Super is Mohandas Gandhi
Nonviolence he won the fight
Super is Nelson Mandela
The Afrikan still burning light
Super is Haili Selassie
The power the Holy might
If you want to call a man
Super
Just get your super right
Don't make up one
Already made super
Just log on to their site
You will be enlightened

BLACK PEARL

Precious and pure
The rarest kind
Put into this world
Upon the Afrikan coast line
Behold the virgin girl
Stolen and stacked
In the hold
On a pirate ship
Call
Black pearl
The most valuable treasures
Have ever been stole
In the history of the whole
Brand new world
A living treasure
Much better than gold
Afrikan virgin girl
The greatest robbery
Have never been told
A ship stock full
Of beautiful black pearl
Sold and molded
To nourish
America new world
Cream of the crops
Arrived at the dock
Stock
Upon a ship name pearl
Afrikan virgin girl
The rarest

Being sold
In the American
New world
Precious and pure
Rarest

BRIDGE TO AFRIKA

Many bridges to cross
Back to the land
Of Ethiopia
The land that bears the cross
Formally name Abyssinia
The country
Where the holy ark
Not lost
Houses the church of orthodox
Children of the prophet
That is not false
Stand down the Italian
Iron tanks
From the back
Of a little white horse
Cushite battle lions
Stand firm
Could not be toss
Every soldier touch
The front line
Bore the Holy Cross
They didn't know
That he was divine
Their chief commanders
Boss
Every raging river

He find
He built a bridge across
The conquering lion
Judah
The Most High ever endorse
Afrika keep flying
Many rivers to cross

Big boat

A big boat
Will sail one day
And it will come
From far, far away
headed for a place
Where there is no
Night or day
Passing through one time
Going one way
A colorful ship
If I must say
Name is positive
And to sail upon
Positive
Is the price you pay
Good will be the order
Given to all each day
Fed by pride
Only the proud knows
We did not come here to stay
Fueled by faith
Faith is the only energy
That will last
The whole way
Navigated by love
Love is the direction
We all must pray
Destination Zion
Positive proud faithful good people
Will live forever together
Upon Jah-meant day

BATTERS UP

Selassie I
He comfort I
Hold I
When eye cry
Brings I up
When I'm let down
He always
Be around
Keeps my heart sound
24 hours long
And guess what?
My king skin is brown
He is the greatest noun
Will make Babylon frown
Bring her down
Pound her down
And her clowns
Up under her scarlet gown
Will be turned around
Locked out of town
Kicked in the ground
Never to be heard
Found
Caped
With the Trinity Crown
Selassie I
Is on the mound
Staring down

BACK THAT HOLDS THE WALL

Our backs are up against the wall
No system for an ex-slave to call
In America the walls are starting to fall
In Afrika I don't think they like us all
We turn our backs when we heard
King Marcus call
Now our black is up against the wall
And any day now the blackness is going to fall
Come down upon us like darkness did Saul
There will be no help in the houses of Paul
Or the idol image hanging on the wall
Black man we had it all, but we turn our backs
When we hear King Marcus call
Now our backs are up against a white wall
Leaning
Broken
And ready to fall
Remember
When Marcus Garvey
Called

MULE AND A FREE MAN

Forty acres
And a mule
But never given
A single tool
A grain of corn
Or
A day in school
No money to start with
But given
The Jim Crow rules
Was it
From the heart
Or just being cruel
Backed
In the plantation
For work
Just like the planned
Fooled
Without money
School
Seed tool
You couldn't feed yourself
None the less an old damn mule
But we survive the heat
And now
Where cool
Most of us lost
The forty acres and the mule
But our children are now
Going to school
Learning and teaching

How to sow seed
And to think
Use our own tools
Give us back
Out forty acres
Now
But free
Them old damn mules

ALL HEART DADDY

Little engine
Big part
A true conqueror
From the start
Man in image
Lion in heart
Solomon in wisdom
The son in smart
Rightful owner
Of the whole world
Mart
Little engine
Big part
Hail king Selassie I
For he is
All heart
It is not the frame
One
Wisdom observes
But the meaning
Of the art
H.I.M

AFRIKAN DESCENT

I am of Afrikan descent
But my body
Have been lent
To a country
That was not content
With the way the world went
They was to relent
And did not want
Their backs bent
They sat down and invent
A way to kick back
And make a few cent
To get rich
Was their intent
Off of the Afrikan descent
Now our jungles are cement
And we are stuck here
Paying rent
The masters
Have not yet repent
After leaving
So many lives bent
X slaves Afrikan descent

ABEL BODY

How long
Will the wicked man reign
While the good man
Bares the cross
And suffers all the pains
Why must it be
This way boss
When will you take
The scene
So much prophets
Have been lost
There is no help
For real human being
The only prophets
Left here are false
And their treatment
To us
Are hateful and mean
It seems like the good
Will always
Pay the cost
For the evil
Children of Cain
Until the return of Abel
Upon the holy white horse
And take away Cain
Insane reign
And bring back the true prophesy
The good that we have lost
Take away all the pain
Restore the barer of the cross

Bring help to us human being
So that our father
Adam
Will no longer pay the cost
For our wicked brother Cain; when will we be Abel again
When will the righteous reign

WHATS UP FAM

Brothers and sisters
We are falling
Apart
It seems like
For each other's
We have no heart
Brother scheming
On brothers
They say
He thinks
That he's so smart
Sisters speaking negatively
Jealousy and envy
Toward one another
The love we needs to carry on
In side
Have not yet
Been discovered
We must let this hate
Be gone
And show compassion
Toward each other
Rich poor cursed saved
We are sisters we are brothers
We have suffered
The same past remember
We fought hate side by side together
And now
How can we hate one another
After what we have been through
Sister brother
How can we now

Fight each other
You are my sister you are my brother
We have turn our backs
Our mothers father

VILLAGE HOME

There is no bosses
In the village
Very few losses
In the village
Children playing
Does not cost us
In the village their little hearts
Never found frost
In the village
Time spent around
Playing horses
In the village
There is no corner
To contact sources
In the village
Not in the malls
Stealing flosses
Or wearing bling
Diamond laces crosses
In the village
There is no bosses
Only the love of a parent
And one love endorses
All in the village

TOOT THE HORN

Dem kick him
With dem boot
But him kick dem back
And him shoot
Dem tried to take
Him fruit
Run him country down
And loot
Dem thought that him was
Mute
That him didn't give a
Hoot
Operated like a
Brute
And him culture was
Pollute
But him wears the conquerors
Suit
And him is king Solomon's Root
And him backed down
The people of the boot
Put down their arms
Them salute
Selassie is the truth
H/is
I/mperieal
M/ajesty
Shoot

THE STUDENT

Hey Mr. cop
Why did you shoot
My brother down?
I know he did not
Do anything wrong
He was on his way
To the holy church to pray
And sing in a gospel song
What did he do so bad
To make you shoot him down?
He never smoke or drink
All he ever did
Was read and think
Or what guilt
Have he been found
He never sold drugs
He never hung out with thugs
But in his head
There is your slugs
He always had a job
He never steal or rob
Now he is lying
Dead on the ground
Why did you shoot my brother
Officer
Why did you shoot him down?
Just today he was fitted
For his diploma cap and gown
Why did you shoot my brother
Mr. cop
What did he do so wrong

SUCCEED YOU

Mama your daughters
Needs you
Show your daughters
How to please you
Show your daughters
How to succeed you
Show your daughters
How to read you
Show your daughters
How to lead true
Mama your daughters
Needs you
Show your daughters
How to plead threw
Show your daughters
How to heed you
Show your daughters
How the seed grew
Show your daughters
How to feed you
Show your daughters
How the weed grew
Mama mama
Your daughter needs you
Tell her to let the breed through
Mama
Your daughters succeeds
You

STEP CHILD

Home good home
Is the place
I yearn to be
My mind have seldom roam
Far, far
Beyond the sea
Sometimes it seems I'm doom
This place here
Can't satisfy me
I feel my spirit will always gloom
As long as I'm in
This slave hell country
Most of my brother
And sister are loom
And the rest say
They're happy
They have money
But no equality
We are the step children
It is like
A bad marriage sadly
The bride is fighting the groom
We must divorce
This house of one sided love
And build our
True love home
A sweet home

SAME ROAD DREAM ROAD

There is this road
That I dream of
Every day
This road I dream
Is paved
In great memories
I might say
And have only yet
To have been traveled
On one way
Some says
It is history
And it should never be traveled
Again
To walk this road
Dread you must be
A price you will pay
Many are searching
For this road
Remembering
We did not come to stay
On this road
There are tears
Drops of human blood shed
And lots of good men
Stand up for right
Tried their might
Some lost their heads
Women and the little girls
Was made drunk
And put into their beds

It is said this road
Runs deep
Into our past history
It have been paved
In hate
From the very first stone
And will remain
As hate
To the very last curve
This road
We needs to travel
Is a very cold
And a hard road
But must
Be traveled back one day
No road have ever been paved
This way
To be traveled
On only one way
For all whom overstand
To say
I and I
Did not come to stay
Knows the truth
And will be one day
Traveling up
That same old road way
Trotting and chanting
Holy be he or she
Whom walks
The kings highway
In my dream
This road is long
In my memory

But very short
And all whom traveling
Upon this road
Bless they will be
And the time it will be
Same time as it was
Of LOT
Same road, dream road

PHOTOGRAPHICALLY

The eye in the tree
Keep on looking at me
Trying to show me something
I just cannot see
I wonder if it is
A sight
From way back
In history
Or could it be
A light
That shines on slavery
When I stare on it
At night
It gives me visions
From across the sea
And when I look at it
Uptight
I see so much pain
Misery
Acorn wooden history
Written in the eyes
In the old oak tree
400 hundred years
Photographically
Staring
Back at me

KINGS DAY

Days of the King
Are drawing
Getting nearer
Song are being sang
The peoples not hearing it
Bells and cries rang
The leaders don't care
Warning to us
It brings
With sign not compared
Vision of the last string
A holy angel's weeping tear
The lion the dragon
A beast
That have wings
The end to the numbers
That evil should fear
The days of the king
Is drawing getting near
Songs are being sang
People listen
Up and hear
To the message that it bring
People listen
Up and hear
Revelation bells
As it rings
Oh people listen
Up and hear
Days of the king
Love and prepare

GULLAH

I chase
Some of my words
But some
I gives it to you
Straight
Erase some of my
Verbs
Some I just debate
Embrace all my
Nouns
With love never no hate
Adjective
I keep low
When working on my faith
Pronoun
I will show
There is no designate
My adverbs
Take it slow
And I anticipate
The words that I know
Gullah
I love and appreciate
I will never let them go
It came
From someone great

GOLD

Hold fast to faith
Marcus Garvey said
The pride
Of the Afrikan people
Is not yet
Dead
Remember your colors
The green the black the red
Remember our home land Afrika
And to Afrika
Our children must be lead
The land of milk and honey
Where the first black family
Was cultured and bred
It is a continent
Not a country
And to this earth body
It is the head
A place where angels worked
In the days
When Jah was feared
We must go back
For what it is worth
To restore the might
The dread
Whole fast to faith
Marcus Garvey said
Our land is green our people is black
And the blood
We have bled is red gold

FOUNDATION

When will we reach the top
We have been
On the bottom
So long
From the days of slavery
It seems
On the bottom
Our level of living
Have stop
We have been in America
Longer than all
Except two races
How come our position
Is still at the bottom
Of the place
We built the foundation
And that is where we lie
Four hundred whole years later
When will we rise
From the ghetto floors
And back to the river Nile
Here we are still
Being used and abused
And for all of our good works
We are still not being
Recognized
Is there something in this country
That is designed
To hold us back
Is it that we have built this country
But did not build it

For us blacks
How can
A mighty race of people
Be held down for so long
In the back
We have got to reach the top
One day
Because we are already holding
The whole country up
From the ground

COTTON FOUNDATION

Cotton exchange
Was the deal
That was arrange
Crops of the mange
No one wanted
To feel that pain
The throne of the white
Be behind it
There was a gain
$$$$$$$$
Look to the blacks
3/5 human being
That we can train
They bleeds blue blood
Through their vain
Let's make them slaves
And we will reign
In the united states of America
That is how

It all begin
3/5 human being
But sane

A SLAVE LIKE I

You ignored
The book of Moses
And took us through slavery
You ignored
The plague
You ignored
The killing of the first born
You ignored
The opening of the red sea
You ignored
The forty years of desert misery
You ignored
The writing of 'the ten commandment' policy
You ignored
The disappearing of the prophet Moses
You ignored
The teaching of the prophet Joshua
You ignored
7000 years of written history
To bring my people to slavery
Jesus Christ the prophet Muhammad
And now
You're ignoring
The king of kings
Haile I Selassie I
The power and the might of the holy trinity
Well I guess
You can ignore
A slave like I

BLACK WINGS

I heard a crow said something
But I didn't understand
What it had said
Then it said it again
And I thought
It was all in my head
He said his name was Jim
And he's working for the fed
Things are going to he changing
Around here
So listen
Before you wines up dead
If you're black
And if I catch you running
I'm aiming for the head
If you're black
And get catch stealing
You're going to be lynched
Until you're red
If you're black
And get catch rapping
Your whole damn family
Will come up dead
If you're black
And get catch learning
I'll burn your barn
And homestead
That I just wanted you all to know
My name is Jim
I am the law
And that was all

I heard from the crow
Then he flew away
And I thought
Was that so?

BACK YARD

In my back yard
I sit
I listen and meditate
I look around
I see
The land that grow
My grandfather great
The scenes that seals
My grandmother faith
It always reminds me
Of the love
Not the hate
1966 late
I give thanks and appreciate
For all the things they've done
And still do
Great
Like the flowers they planted
In my back yard
Every year it blossoms
And something great
Comes new
In my back yard grandma grandpa
Your love
And your presence

You're still coming through
We love you tooo!

THE PROMISE

Forgive I Jah
For my people
Have forgotten
About the ship that sailed
From so far away
And
About the promises
We made to our race
To never go astray
Always remain faithful
To our home land
Afrika way
Never to give our heart
Away to our capturer
Never to follow
What he say
In his wicked and foul ways
Don't forget
So soon my people
It was just
400 years ago
We all were just black slaves
Analyzing
Our whole accomplishment
In the last
One hundred years

Not much have came
From all
That we have gave
We should know by now
The time has come
To stand up
And take hold
Of our own
The only way
For love to happen
Realizing that Afrika
Is our home
It is there we should
Give our self-respect
And honor within our own
The time is now over
For us to be
Down under
And this brand new time
Have come
For us to rise
Above
And remember
The most important
Promise
In your heart
There is only space
For Afrika
One true love
You promise

THE MASTER SLAVE

Brought and taught
Knows how to behave
Stay in spot
Need not be brave
One black dot
Hallelujah i am save
Black on black plot
Take and never gave
The kettle
And the pork laced pot
False waves
Clean cut shave
Just being
Whom you're not
Number one nigger
The uncle and aunt tom crave
Look back
Did not see
Lot
Pepper didn't follow salt
To the grave
Wake up
That side of the pillow
Is getting hot
The master slave
The house nigger
Only knows what
He has been taught
And bought
For $lave

SOLID

Predictionary
Mr. Webster one and two
Told me
The meaning of black
Now eye can see
Why we're all in the back
Nigroid pack
Dirty and slack
Wicked by his facts
Evil and crack
A deed is black
Disaster dishonor
A look is black
A mood is black
Calamitous
Opposite being white
Everything about black
He defined not right
Except darkness
From whence
Out came his light
Mr. Webster
Forget the most important
Element of black
The people are beautiful
The enlightening

SLAVERY DAY

Slavery day
Should be celebrated
In a special way
Without shame or hate
If just to say
Thanks
To our grands and greats
For four hundred years
Of humiliating work
Without pay or pardon
We did not lose
A day of faith
Four hundred years
Slave mindedly obeyed
Their commands and demands
For 21 generations straight
One day
It should not be delayed
Not for another
May be
The celebration
Should be celebrated
For the black the blue the gray
Together
We are 142 years late
Slavery day wake

SHORE TO SHORE

Jah, Jah
Don't let my ship sink
I'm down
On my knees
Trying to break
This last link
And caught up in a freeze
Oh my god it's hard to think
If i could just have them keys
We are in the eye
And it won't blink
A hurricane breeze
This ship is sailing
On instinct
And we are in a squeeze
On the deck down below
Where it is jam pack
And inhumanly link
Jah please help us to shore
The seas have swell
Please Jah, Jah
Make it shrink
We are not to be
Celled
Please make dem think

ROCKING SHIPS

Hold tight my brothers
Never let go
Hold tight
My sisters
Let love truly show
Take a worldly grip
And reach higher up
For mo'
500 years
Off the ships
We have hardly left the shore
Remember
Our big Afrikan nose-lips
Self-knowledge
We then knew
The plan to flip
The slave master ship
And return
To Afrikan shore
Hold tight
My brothers
My sisters
And never let it
Go
Just let your Afrikan love
Show
Hold tight
To the shore

PART TWO

My great grand father
Was brought here
As a slave
Worked every day
Of his life
Until he met his grave
Across his back
Is where
He got his pay
Scarred and branded
In his skin
But we are still
Afrikan men
The leader set us free
But the people
Did not agree
They took him off the stand
And replaced him
With a president
Of whom
Did not even ran
But I'm still an
Afrikan man
They said if we follow
The north star
We will be protected
By our brothers
From the civil war
Some did all they could
One thing we didn't know
In the ghetto
There is no land
But I'm still an Afrika man

OPPORTUNITY TRAPP DOOR

Where is the black rights
To humanity
Hidden behind the trapp door
Where is the black man
In the declaration of independency
Hidden behind the trapp door
Where is the black man
In the constitution be
Hidden behind the trapp door
Where is the black man
In the equal amendment agree
Hidden behind the trapp door
Where is the black man
In the law of justice key
Hidden behind the trapp door
Where is the black man
In liberty
Hidden behind the trapp door
Where is the black man
In white society
Hidden behind the trapp door
Where is the black man
In the united states free
Hidden behind the trapp door
Where is the black man
Memory
Hidden behind the trapp door

NORTH STAR TO THE EAST

North star you have guided my people
To freedom before
Now will you guide us to freedom once more
Our journey is to the east
And the travel is much far over the great ocean
And back to Afrika our grandparent told us long time ago
To get to freedom, we must travel by night
And follow your lights
And by day
Stay out of sight
They said to the north
Was the land of the free
And the people up there
Are living under equal rights
Liberty
But now we see
It was to balance
The blacks in the country
Most of us are now in the ghettos
Of the cities
The end
The bottom
Which they are using
As holding pens
For the prisons and penitentiaries
Back in to slavery again
Only now set up
Voluntarily
So now we know
Our freedom is to the east
From whence we came

We must go in order to break this leash chains
and your guiding north star
We look unto once more
We shall see you by faith
We will follow you by day
And when the sun sets
We all will pray
Then lay low
We will stay on the same trail back
That our mothers and fathers
Traveled before
Until our soul reaches upon Afrikan shores
To freedom everlasting
To freedom forever more
We wish upon your lights
North star
And to the east will the ocean current flow

NEW DEVICE

Chain cutter
Come and cut me free
I have been chained down
For three or more centuries
It was first
Around my ankles
And pain ran up to my knees
It left such a scar
Back there
I thought
I would never live again
Free
But the day came
They cut the chains
That was holding back
My ankle and knees
But at a price
A new device
One that the eyes couldn't see
It was still a chain
But on my brain
Started in elementary
Teaching me names
And past history
But not a word
Was taught about me
Now I am locked
In another man's time
Still waiting
In the 21st century
Waiting for the chain cutter

To come and cut me free
But i warn you chain cutter
These chains
You cannot see

MIGHTIER THAN THE PEN

Natty dread ride again
Packing lead
And sling the pen
In a war
To get the hungry fed
And the innocent
Out from the guilty pen
Battling
On the written line
Using its head
Drawing enemy into friend
Turning stone hate
Into water and bread
Freeing the lions
From the den
Helping the trying
Before hope dread
Stop the dying
In zones coded red
He is from Zion
He is natty dread
He is a lion
From the psalm of his head
There is no denying
He rides in the wind
On his side

A pencil and a pen
Good man hold tight
Natty dread ride again
In this Armageddon
He write
And your word
Will read the end
Natty dread ride again

BIG OR SMALL

Big Wheeler
That you are
You drive
A big fancy car
You smoke
A big thick cigar
You sit up big
In the bar
Think that's big
Is what you are
The biggest thing
So far
Big ego who saw
Big ring
On your paw
Big stakes
You eat raw
Always bigger
Never a draw
So much bigger
Than the law

I wonder
Who they think you are
Biggie Smalls

BORROW

My days are full
With sorrow
I can't wait to see
What bring my tomorrow
It seems
My TIME is being
Borrowed
My life is just
Full
With the down and low
And I'M watching
The whole thing
From the crack
Of the broken window
While a sad song
Is being sang
By a lonely sparrow
Every lyric it brings
Pierces my heart
With a silver arrow
This world I live in
Hollow
It's space so lonely so
Narrow
I can't wait to see
What bring my tomorrow

Because tonight
I have only my sorrow

CRY IT

It is and order
For I
To write what eye cry
Document
Hates and lies
Note down
That I try
Send letter
To the most high
Sketch
What my eyes
Draws
To tell me why
Trace
No one that die
Print
My piece of pie
Broadcast
Selassie I
Up to the most high

.

FATHER SON

The truth
Is free
The lie
Is captivity
The truth about me
It is that
I am truly free
I agree
With the Holy Trinity
And what I should be
Son of Selassie
Truly free

HIS WAY

One of these days
Mark
What I say
Gonna get it my way
Gonna Get Pay
On the top
My way
High hop to stay
No instruction
To obey
Hood production
Everyday
O.K.
Peace direction
Problems
Kept at bay
Love perfection
Get it my way
Prayer protection
One of these days
Mark
What I say
Here to stay

LEAD AND LOVE

My pencil
Is my lady
She always make me right
My pencil is my baby
I sleep with it a night
We wrap
Together tight
Creates poetry from out of sight
And rhymes it all up
Perfectly right
A special day card
Love letters and songs
That breaches the feelings height
Political thoughts
Just comments
But never eye write to fight
My pencil is my lady
She draws me happy
When I'M uptight
She is my dear sweet baby
Together in love
We create written light
She correct my wrong
Makes my write

ONE DAY

Thank you Jah
Rastafari
You have been good to me
Today
Is the same tomorrow
I will be satisfied
All stumbling blocks
Was cast away
I saw your lights
It kept bright
My way
Thank you Jah
For a wonderful day

REAL AND ROD

HIM
HIM a King
HIM A Lord
HIM the conqueror
Lion from Judah
HIM everything
HIM A God
HIM got more wisdom
Mt. Buddha
HIM got wings
The bow of Nimrod
HIM knows the others
The Intruders
Unto HIM
We sing
A joyful noise
With HIM we trump
And trod
HIM is the lion of Judah
The king of kings
The Lord of Lords
In peace
HIM carries a rod
H.I.M
God

SOUR LINES

Writer's digest
Gave me
A written test
Ask me
Where did I get this mess
If I
Came from out the west
Don't settle for the less
Can I
Put on a suit and vest
That I
Have found a written chess
Would I
Come out to see their nest
And I
Needed to confess
Can I
Sign this request
Dog, I am the very Best
I, and I
Readers Can't digest
Oh
What a Filthy Mess
They keep on bringing it
Right back up
All over the place

THE OLD HOUSE

My mother is
A Christian
Oldest sister is
A Muslim
I and I
A Rastaman
To complete
The third mission
To cast out
All the hoodlums
Of whom
Those not overstand
For man
I and I
A gone fishing
To reason
With the wise
And the rude one
May magnificence
Be your bliss
And heavenly be your land
In Zion
There is no dream
And no need
Forever wishing
My oldest sister is
A Muslim
I and I am Rastaman
My mother is
A Christian
And our future joins us all
To our Father Abraham

LIGHT

Now you are
The light of my life
It is you whom
Brightens up my days
And at night
You guide my way
In the morning
Beside you
I kneels and pray
And in the evening
It is
I love you
I can't wait to hear
You say
All I do
Is think of you
I dangles in your rays
The things you do
Tells me you're true
Love works
Always pays
It keeps me light up
All the TIME
Winter TIME
Feels like May
You see
You are inside
My mind
And in your heart

Is where my heart stays
I love you
And in your trust
Is where my burdens lays
The light of my life
Ok

THE TOMASSES

My nephews
Calls me uncle Tommy
My enemy calls me Tom
But I will hit you
In the mind
Rapp riddles
And my Rhymes
Stand you up
In line
Straighten up your knees
Your spine
Take away that nine
Throw down
Your whiskey wine
Put you up
On pine
Tattoo on
A bright peace sign
Get your true love on the grind
Move you forward
Into humankind
Yes
My nephews calls me
Uncle Tommy
That's fine

Me enemy calls me Tom
They're blind
But I don't care
Who is who
Because it's all
Just a matter of TIME
Uncle Tom
No family of mine

TURN BACK

We took the wrong turn
When they told us
We were free
Instead of heading back
Home to Africa
We stayed and was resold
Into a life
Of unjust and misery
Black men and black women
We took the wrong turn
Our neighborhoods
Are called the bottom
In every town
In every city
We should have had
Went to the east
We choose to stay
In the west
All we've gotten is hate
And hate test
Still they have no pity

For us
We were at the crossroad
With an IMPORTANT
Decision to make
We could have went
Back home we thought
That would be a mistake
Now we are still here marooned
And the backs
Of our African spirits
Have brake
We took the wrong turn
My people
The whole of us are lost
We need to be turned around
To seek
What is in the other direction
Is down
America is a beautiful place
We started out here
Tiling the ground
Now our people have so many faces
All were doing here
Right now
Is being INTIMATES
Jokers and clowns
Might I say my people
From the day we were free
That turn we took
Was wrong

UNREST

We are in the west
Put daily
Through the test
Looking at wrongly
Clearly
As the lest
In neighborhoods filled
Of rats
Roaches and human
Pest
Living in the robbers nest
Born into
The ghetto mess
The street lives wild
No sleep no rest
Our babies
Are not even safe
In the public schools desk
Brothers getting cases
Like doing TIME
Is now a new quest
Sisters love
Is some TIME wasted
But hang in there girl
Do your very best
Our family reunion
Use to be the fest
Now it is a funeral
We are daily departed
There is no peace there is not rest
Yes

We are still in the west
Our struggles begins
And it ends
From our birth
Into our death
Unrest in the west

WAIT DON'T HATE

I endite
This verse
I was sold
Now they say
I am curse
Lost my weight in gold
Now I have no worth
They say
That I am cold
Gives them black
Vision of a Hurst
But I am in a hole
And I've been there
Ever since birth
A white hole
And it is full to the top
With hate
Unfairness and wrath
Out of control
Waiting for me
To brake or burst
Trying to keep my soul
But Jah, Jah
Got there first
I am whole
One with the universe

WE HAVE PAID THE WAY

Free Spirit
Captive mind
A condition
In heart
From the slave master wine
Now
A fool's education
To keep us self-blind
Dedication and donation
To this country
Define
Through the plantation
Came millions
And us
Not a DIME
Our
Separation in desegregation
As a whole
We have fallen behind
Free spirit
Release your mind
Your future inherit
From a pass that
Emulated divine

WHO IS THE WIFE

You are not
My father brother
Why should I
Call you uncle
My uncle is my father's keeper
And their mother
Are the same
You are not
A family to me
Using my cousins, brothers, and sisters
To play dirty war games
Then turn around
Your back on them
When they returns home
Shaken broken lame
We scratch each other's back
In our old house
Our grand fathers
Are the same
I will not
Be calling you uncle
My uncle and I
Are the same team
And our pictures
Are in the same frame
Mr. Sam

CORN

Hail to the Chiefs
Whom founded
This great nation
Long before we came
Civilization
And started our
Congregation
To this great place
You are the foundation
You planted the first seeds
And taught
The first education
And unto the first born
You were the first
In celebration
You marked the place
That would be
The greatest
In world communication
And in the war
Your language
Was a most inspiring dedication
And unto the great spirit
You are the first
In meditation
Hail to the chiefs
Of this great nation
You are the foundation

Long before we came
Civilization
And started our
Congregation
To this great place
You are the foundation
You planted the first seeds
And taught
The first education
And unto the first born
You were the first
In celebration
You marked the place
That would be
The greatest
In world communication
And in the war
Your language
Was a most inspiring dedication
And unto the great spirit
You are the first
In meditation
Hail to the chiefs
Of this great nation
You are the foundation

CLEAN WASH

I will fight
For my right
To be free
In my plight
To always be in
Jah's light
Black history
Is my might
In slavery
Took my sight
Brain washed me
Vampire bites
Now I can see
My day was night
I found the keys
Strapped to a kite
Electricity and elementary
Thunder and light
Fools money
Took our sight
My mind is free
Now I will flight
For the truth
And for my right
Now
Brothers and sisters
Stand firm
Hold tight

COTTON SEED

Sixteen hours a day
Working in the cotton field
Oh my God we pray
As the sun burns
Ours back begin to peel
How much longer
Will we pay
For this wicked, wicked, cotton deal
Getting around thorns
And snakes all day
When it's all through
All you can do is kneel
Sometime if you don't obey
All day
You go to bed without a meal
If you ever try to run away
Your master
Will cut off your toes
And leave you
With just a heel
Whenever you are around the house nigger
Be sure
To keep your lips sealed
Because every word you say
Like a pig
The house nigger will squeal
And you get a whip
Across your back
Until you cannot feel
Four hundred years of slavery
Was real

We must keep on writing
Our stories must be revealed

HE LIVES

David
Was the living God
And his roots still stand today
It is real
That his kingdom
Will reign forever
And his son's
Will forever lead the way
Coming through the lion of Judah
The last son
Will come to stay
He will rid the world
Clean of it wrong
Give thanks and praises
Unto the living God
We must all
HE lives!

GREATER THAN MY I

Kunta Kinte
Never ran away
He was running to
He was taken away
To a place
He couldn't stay
He was SIMPLY going home
To whom he obey
A straight African warrior
To the very last day
We ran away
And now we are left
Astray
Afraid to say
The name Kunta Kinte
He was right
As an African he prayed
For us the African to pray
To sop running away
From our roots
Thank you
Mr. Hailey Kunta Kinte

EARTH WIDE

Third world people
Jah
Is by your side
Don't you be afraid
Hold on to your pride
Grow your dreads
Braids
And don't you ever hide it
Don't let your colors fade
Or push it to the side
It is the way
We have been made
And it should never
Be denied
Captain of the deck
Is the Ace of Spade
When it's on board
The queen does
The shuffle
The king does
The slide
The jokers dem hides
Third world people
African
Sold and trade
We are not on vacation
But we are world wide
Third world people
Third world pride
Afrikan abide

DREAD EYE MAN

Return
Of the dread eye man
HIM sees
And him over stand
HIM listen
To the Rasta-man Band
HIM say
Why dem a fight
Over HIM land
How did this country became
Drug over ran
Dem cover up everything
Before the-----hits the fan
No food
For the poor country
The ghetto man's pan
Rich forks
A run to their secret land
For sun
Say it's for dem tan
Segregation hate
Will bring an end to
Human
Welcome home
The dread eye man
HIM sees and him understand
All the sins
Is not a part of HIM plan
It is TIME for good
To take a good stand
Love is our right
Our demand

The dread eye man
Sees
Long as the land
HIM came through
Our GREAT grand
The dread eye man
HIM seen
The promised land Eye sees

DOG TALK

Corner a cat
It will come out
Scratching
Corner a rat
It will go down
Snitching
Sketching
The cat will
Combat
Leave you behind
Patching
The rat will
Be down town
Matching
That cat will keep
Its mouth shut
When it receives
It latching
The rat will deny it
Talking
But it will keep on
Fetching

FAMILY STAR

I can't be a star
Without JAH
I lights won't shine too far
I can't be a star
Without my PA
Who's going to
Pat my shoulder
Yes sir
No star
Without mama
AH, AH
Where will I get my
Last supper
No SUH
Can't be a star
Without brother
Keeper
Who's going to keep my back cover
No SUH
There's no star
Without sister
AH, AH
Who's going to help me
To know to check my lover
HA, HA No SUH
Can't be a star
With Rasta
Who's going to be there
Musically directing war
No Suh
Can't Be

Without loving fans
No SUH AH, AH
Who's going to be there
When I take
The Grand Stand
Yes SUH
Can't Be A Star
Without JAH
My Lights
Wouldn't shine to far
Can't Be

FOR MOTHER

Dear Mother Africa
Since we left
Out from your gardens
We have traveled
In many new spaces
Nothing yet
Have we found
That could equal
To your grace
You birth the first
Of all existence
Your development
Have kept it pace
You labored the birth
Of all human race
Different revelation religion
Different color of face
But it all started
At big Mama's place
Dear Mama
Home should be
Where our heart is
But right now
Our minds
Have gone in outer spaces
And it is so hard to find
A stepmother
With your gardens
And your grace
My Dear Mother
Race

FRONTY

You and I
Need money
Dog
To make our lyric fly
We need
Helping fronty
Dog
To help us pass
This by
This mess we're in
Not so funny
Dog
Gotta stand up to it
Gotta try
Foot by charm
For the bunny
Dog
Luck or skills
We can't deny
These streets need it
Like honey
Dog
Headed into the sky
Cloudy days soon be sunny
Dog
But now
We be just getting by
Waiting for the hope
The dream
That fronty

Dog
So funny
Dog
Don't cry
You and I
Need money
Dog
Make them lyric
High fly
I and you
Needs money
Dog
This mother ship
Must fly

ILLEGALIZERS

I write this poem
To all of the people
Who are responsible for the illegalization
Of the herb
Let it grow
It is the healing of the nation
And the illegalizers know
Green it is fresh
And there are many different kind
Guarantee you will walk fine
No dizziness over hang
Like whiskey, beer and wine
Straight in the morning
Smoke one
Off to business on TIME
Without the hang over
Because last night you smoked pine
Free as a bird feeling fine
You see illegalizers
It's about TIME
For you to wake
Up and smell the kind
Remove the drunken hate
Cigarette, whiskey, beer and wine
And replace it with
Green love like mine
Some call it Gunja
Some call it pine
Illegalizers
You've got to over stand
That stuff you've got legal

Brings out
The hate in man
A dizziness out of the bottle
Over standing
Bud out of the land
Out from a garden
Some are still in the closet
A little dirt
A little water light in an old pan
The original best friend
Women and men
Food for the brain
Out from the dirt
Into a pipe pan
Roll it up
In between
There is no demand
Out of the earth
Part of the master's plan
Illegalizers
It is for you to over stand
The tree that you are barking
Is the original herb for a man
As long as man is here on earth
This weed will grow spring
Stand
All of the singer and leaders of the bands
Relate these words to your
Non-smoking weed fans
Legalize herb
It will legalize man

LAND FOR WE

I am not a saint
You see
I am simply
Meant to be
I know my past
History
I came from Africa
Into Slavery
There is nothing special
About me
Simply want to help
Set my people free
We have been here
For four whole century
We built this whole
Damn country
Now we just want
All to see
That we know our A/B and C's
And we can count
Two more than three
We don't want
The presidency
No part of
The dirty money
We just simply
Want to be
Truly free
To go back home To our country
Africa free
A land for we

LABOR NO FAVOR

You flood the nation
With African
To see your work
Be done
You never paid
Not a one
Now that the days
Of slavery is gone
You look at us
In a scorn
Low pay and no pay
Can't get any loan
I guess our TIME
Have come and gone
But you still need
Your dirty work done
But don't want
To pay us none
Instead of inviting
Over African
For pay
So you can help
Back our nation
You open the gates
For the Mexican
Brother I don't hate
On your colorful nation
But brother watch your faith
When you become an American
Your colors Don't carry Weight
We are black African
Thank you Jah
For the wisdom

You have invested in I and I
Thank you Jah
For the children
You have given to I and I
Thank you Jah
For my great parent
Whom pampered me in my cries
Thank you Jah
For my sibling
Share the same rest place
Days and month by and by
Thank you Jah
For my aunts and uncles
Whom I will never deny
Thank you Jah
For all my cousins
Being there for I and I
For all of my friends
We will always be fun tied
Thank you Jah
For all this wonderful
Earth
To live life peaceful and die
Happy
For the eyes to see
Our king is the royal
Haili Selassie I
I and I thank you Jah, Jah
To the most high
For my ancestors whom
Kept your lights
From the dark lies
Thank you Jah

STOLEN CASE

Elementary my dear
It *don't* take
a microscope to see
This investigation
Is history
Slavery
The number one element
In this cold case story
Made billions
For this country
Brought over millions
In total misery
Totaling trillions
In American property
This case is closed
Insanity
The judge already knows
It's a hung jury
Just
Ice
My dear
It's elementary

REFUGEE

We did not come
Through Ellis Island Doors
We were not refugees
And we were not Starving
or ran From our country
We lived Among the harvesting tree
Where fresh waters sprung
And all is free
From Africa To slavery
We did not arrive
Through the Ellis Island entry
But now we are
Refugee

.

POSITION

How the west was won
A lot of killing
A lot of gun
Blood spilling
and
Lying on the son
Amen
Wicked dealing
Land stealing
Treaty breaking
Lives taken
Church faking
Chief forsaken
Race hating
Power misused
Country abuse
The west was never won
It was simply
Possessed

MASTER PLAN

Bridges are built
Bridges are burned
The verdict is guilt
The Babylon
Have not yet learn
In the days of Moses
What was Jah most
Important concern
It was the least
And not the most
His good work always
Accrue in
A slave must stand up
To the host
For the respect and honor
His people have earned
Crossing the Atlantic Ocean
All bridges are burned
Looking back
On the days of Moses
Babylon you still
Have not yet learn

LONELY LION

Lonely Lion
Roars
Into the Wind
He is the King of the Pride
Therefore,
He has no Equal,
no friend,
He roams the country sides
The rivers
The hills the dens
Seeking evil
In the places they hides
Putting it to an end
The forces of nature
Is his lead
His guide
For him to bend
Would mean his end
His presence is felt
World wide
He rages the storm
A perfect ten
To be number one
In a lion pride
Means not to be born
But to be sent
Lonely lion roaring
In the wind

Dwelling in places
No mind has ever been
His AIM his destination
Is to bring evil temptation
To be stop
To be end

LIKE THE FIRST

No Rasta
Imposter
You mean to tell me
You know Jah?
Ha-Ha-Ha
Came so far
Have you been living up to par?
Vegetable raw
King David star
Have you stop drinking In the car?
Out the bar
Be a good pa
Savings In your faith jar
Are you giving for tomorrow?
Is that so Rasta
Do you know Rasta
Want to go Rasta
He no Whore Rasta
Want to be Rasta
Trinity Rasta
*Selassie I Rasta
The first to be Rasta
No Imposter
Rasta
*SELASSIE -the power of the trinity

MORE ABOUT THE AUTHOR

Thomas Bryan, JR – 1961 was born in Beaufort County S.C, on Hilton Head Island. He was nurtured by four fathers and five mothers; his grandparents, James Bryan, Jr., Julia Bryan, Freddie Chisolm, and Leotha Chisolm; his parents, Thomas Bryan, Sr, Laura Bryan, and his oldest sister Mumtahanah Abdul-Malik. They all took a meaningful part in molding him into a conscious black man. He grew up working with his father and grandfather on the river harvesting oysters, clams, fish, but most of all, shrimp. Shrimping was the family business. During the seventies, while in his teens, he worked as a line cook for one of many restaurants on the Island. He since married and had three children, who are the lights that keep his light shining. His occupation changed to carpentry which he continues to this day. As his children progressed in age, he found himself with a lot of free time on his hands, so he dedicated his time to an old hobby; writing. One could usually find Bryan and his good friend Bernard Snyder writing poetry. Thomas Bryan, JR is hopeful to be a professional writer/poet turning his "hobby" into his last full-time occupation; (his curiosity).

ACKNOWLEDGMENTS

I would like to give thanks to the greatest Christian I know; a mother to many; my mother, Laura Mae Bryan. She, along with my father, assisted the Creator in giving me life. Next, I would like to give thanks to my father Thomas Bryan, Sr. for making my mother his Holy Wife forever.

Thanks to my dearest sisters and brothers; my keepers; my seven bright trees of light, they are the inspiration to my insight.

Special thanks to Selah M. Bryan, Ellis Clement, and Bernard Snyder; daughter and fellow-poet who inspired my poetic plight. They motivate me to write and write for right.

A special, special thanks to all my blood and Gullah family, my friends, special friend, my whole Hilton Head Island family, and work buddies. Thanks, with love and peace for prosperity.

Last and greatest thanks to Marcus Mosiah Garvey for turning on the eternal lights to the African Library of Black History and directing me to the Might of our King by Roots and Culture Haile Selassie.

Thanks, and praises to the Most High, one love Jah Rastafari.

www.ingramcontent.com/pod-product-compliance
Lightning Source LLC
Chambersburg PA
CBHW080344300426
44110CB00019B/2498
9780692129401